RIGHT

REVISED EDITION

REVISED EDITION

T. B. Maston/ William M. Pinson, Jr.

RiGHT OR WRONG?

A guide for teeners and their leaders for living by Christian standards

Broadman Press/Nashville, Tennessee

4261–16

ISBN: 0-8054-6116-7

Library of Congress Catalog Card Number: 75–143282
Dewey Decimal Classification: 241
Printed in the United States of America

Preface

Do you ever find it difficult to know whether a particular activity is right or wrong? The discussions in this book represent an attempt to set out some basic principles that you can use to decide for yourself what is right and wrong for you to do. These principles are applied in Part II to some of the more common problems of young people.

It has been assumed throughout these discussions that you are an intelligent Christian youth who wants to know what is right and will be willing to search diligently for the right. It also has been assumed that there *is* such a thing as right and wrong, that one can know the right and wrong, and that the right will always be best. The last assumption means that we should search for the right, and once knowing it, we should joyously seek to do it.

Although written primarily for you and other Christian youth, it is hoped that this material will be helpful to your parents, teachers, and leaders.

We trust that you will read carefully Part I on Christian principles before considering the issues in Part II. We also hope that after you have considered prayerfully the issues discussed in Part II you will carefully read the two concluding chapters in Part III.

You should understand that there is no attempt in this book to examine every phase of the Christian life. The discussions are restricted, to a large degree, to issues or problems that we believe are most immediately acute in the lives of Christian young people. There are important areas of the Christian life, more positive in the main, that are not touched on at all. Also, issues such as war, revolution, pollution, poverty, racial prejudice, and other complex social problems are not discussed. These matters or problems are outside the purpose of the present volume.

This book, which was first published in 1955, has been more widely distributed than originally anticipated by the writer or publisher. Also, it has been translated into at least the following languages: Arabic, Chinese, Portuguese, and Spanish.

In the years since the original publication, the problems of young people have changed considerably. The author had a deepening conviction that the book should be revised and updated. Some issues faced by contemporary young people are new, others are more acute or less important than fifteen years ago. The original author asked Dr. Bill Pinson to share in the revision of the book.

May the Lord use these brief chapters to help you find personally satisfying and Christ-honoring answers to the perplexing questions and problems of your life. This is our prayer. Will you not help to answer this prayer by approaching the reading and studying of this book with an open mind and with a heart that is willing to follow any light that may come to you from our heavenly Father?

We acknowledge our indebtedness to many young people and others who have contributed in various ways to this book. We express our appreciation in particular to Mrs. Melvin Bridgford, who prepared the final copy for the publisher.

Unless otherwise indicated, all references to the Scriptures are from *Good News for Modern Man*, popularly referred to as Today's English Version.

T. B. MASTON and
WILLIAM M. PINSON, JR.

Contents

1. Youth and Decisions

You have discovered by now that to live is to make decisions. Have you also noticed that increasingly you are making your own decisions? Formerly you depended largely on parents or some other adult to make decisions for you. If you are like most young people you have longed for the time when you would be free to make your own decisions. You have thought of that as "a wonderful day." It can be a wonderful day, but it will be only if you are adequately prepared for it.

Major Decisions

We shall concentrate in this book on the decisions that you and other young people make in one particular area: the area of right or wrong. Before we come to a specific consideration of "right or wrong," we want to discuss briefly decision making in general. Let us begin with a few suggestions concerning three major decisions. Other decisions may be very important, but we believe that you will agree that these are *the* major decisions of life.

One of these is really *the* major decision of life for all people—children, young people, and adults. Adapting a question found in the Scriptures, it can be stated as follows: "What will you do with Jesus which is called the Christ?" The answer one gives will determine his destiny for this life and for the life to come. Also, the decision concerning one's relation to Christ will color and influence every other decision, including the other two major decisions. If you have not made this destiny-determining decision, we hope you will open your heart and life and invite the resurrected Christ to come in to live.

We assume that you have had this initial Christian experience. You may, however, have lost at times the glow of that experience. If you have wandered away from the Lord and have lost the joy and peace that a Christian should have, will you not right now ask God to forgive you for those things that have come between you and him? Will you not ask him to restore to you a sense of his presence and the strength you need to live victoriously for him?

Another of life's three major decisions is the choosing of your life's work. We have just one life to live; how tragic if we make a mistake with it. One of the most common mistakes made by many young people is simply to drift into their life's work without any intelligent deliberate decision. Do not be unduly disturbed if you have not yet decided on your life's vocation or profession. This is not particularly unfortunate for you at your age. You do need to understand, however, that you are laying the foundation now for the decision you will make later about your life's work.

The third of the major decisions is the choice of a life's companion: the one with whom you will seek to find and fulfil the will of God. This decision is just as important as the one concerning your life's work. It is hoped that you will just as diligently and prayerfully seek the will of God regarding your companion for life as you do for any other area of life. You may not yet have made this decision. You are right now in the process, however, of making decisions that will ultimately shape if not determine that decision.

Related Decisions

Other important decisions are more or less closely related to each of these three major decisions. In some cases these decisions clearly affect the major decisions. Some of these "related decisions" will be discussed in Part II.

Let us first look at some decisions that are related to the choice of a companion. There are decisions that are made previous and subsequent to that decision. For example, what about relations to those of the opposite sex during the dating period, which will be discussed in Part II?

There will also be related decisions after marriage. The wise or right choice of a life's companion does not automatically assure a sound Christian home. Decisions will be made after marriage which will determine the happiness of the members of the family and the contribution of the home to the lives of the members of the family, to the community, and to the church and the cause of Christ. Is it to be a real Christian home or merely nominally Christian? Will there be faithfulness to the church? Will regular family worship be maintained? Will an honest effort be made to show the Christian spirit in relation to one another in the home? What about children that come into the home, will they be dedicated to the purposes of God?

Other important decisions are related to the choice of your life's work. Some of these precede while others follow the decision itself. For example, any decision you make concerning the predominant values and motives in your life will help to determine your decision concerning your life's work. It will make a great deal of difference whether you are primarily concerned with your own advantage, financial and otherwise, or are interested primarily in service to God and your fellowman.

When one has decided his life's vocation, there are other related decisions that will determine how effective he will be in his vocation. Among these are the preparation he makes for his vocation and the discipline he has to work diligently at his vocation. From the Christian perspective there is also the question of the purposes to be served through one's vocation.

Some tremendously important decisions are related to the decision regarding Christ. Most of these are made after we become Christians. They are decisions that a Christian continues to make throughout life. To make it personal, are you going to accept Christ not only as Savior but also as Lord? What kind of a Christian are you going to be: a merely nominal Christian with your name on the church roll and little else? Or, are you going to seek as best you can to be a real Christian? Are you going to make your love for Christ and your devotion to his cause central in your life? To use an athletic term, do you want to play on God's first team? He needs more of us who will give our best for and to him.

If you do not already, will you let your relation to Christ so permeate your life that it will be a decisive factor in the other decisions of life? What about the daily decisions of life, some of which will be discussed in Part II? Are you in the process of making or will you make those decisions in the light of the insights that come from your Christian faith, your relation to Christ, and your devotion to his cause? If your answer is in the affirmative, you are on the way to becoming a real, in contrast to a nominal, Christian.

Decisions: Major and Minor

We have suggested that there are three major decisions. We have also suggested that other decisions are more or less closely related to these major decisions. We want now to suggest that many decisions that seem to be minor may actually be of major importance because of their impact on our lives and on the other decisions we make.

For example, it may not seem important whether you go to college or not, or the particular college to which you will go. There is a possiblity, however, that such a decision will set the whole direction of your life, including the choice of life's companion and life's work and the quality of life you will live for Christ. Even the decision regarding a particular course in school may be potentially very important. It may begin a journey for you that will last throughout your life. It may not seem important whether you read a particular pamphlet or book, go to a specific lecture, attend Sunday School, worship service, or a youth discussion on a particular Sunday, or go to a youth retreat or assembly, but any one of these could be a major factor in molding your life. It may not seem impor-tant whether or not you have a date with a particular individual or whether you attend a particular game or social function. But that which seems unimportant may have significant consequences. The same is true regarding the day-by-day decisions in the area of right and wrong.

Do you remember some occasion when you or your family were making a trip and came to a fork in the road? The two roads may have appeared quite similar. It looked like it would not make much difference which one you took. But that was only surface appearance. At first the roads were only one lane apart, but ultimately they were miles apart. It is like that in life. A decision may seem minor now, but the final outcome may be of major proportions.

Decisions and Destiny

You are in the process of making destiny-determining decisions. They are destiny-determining in more ways than one. One way is the pattern they tend to weave into your life. When decisions are carefully analyzed, they tend to reveal the prevailing motives and purposes of our lives. They will reveal whether we are selfish and self-centered, other-centered, or, on the highest level, Christ-centered.

Certainly no life is as Christ-centered as it should be, but do our decisions reveal that we are moving in that direction? To make it personal, do you have a sincere desire to honor Christ in the decisions you make in every area of your life, including the area of right and wrong? The wonderful thing is that the more life is lived for Christ and others, the richer and happier it will be.

Decision making in our lives is somewhat like the weaving of a tapestry. It is composed of countless threads. What it portrays or symbolizes does not appear clearly until near the end of the weaving. Similarly, the final pattern of our lives may not be clearly evident until near the end. But we can be sure that every thread that has been put into life affects the final product.

When the weaver of the tapestry starts, he has a pattern or visualizes what he wants in the final product. Our heavenly Father is the Master Weaver. He knows what he wants to make of our lives. He has to depend, however, on our co-operation with him. What dream do you have for your life? What do you want it to look like toward the end of the journey, when the tapestry of your life will be near completion? Will the decisions you are making today contribute to that kind of finished product?

2. Levels of Living

Have you recently made a decision concerning alcohol, drugs, sex, or some similar problem? If so, did you do what others were doing, or did you deliberately and intelligently make your own personal decision? Could you have defended the decision you made? If so, what arguments would you have given? Have you developed the maturity, the strength, and the stability to stand by your decisions once you have made them? Can you do this without needlessly offending those who disagree with you?

It will be a great help to you if you have built into your life some fundamental principles that will give you a basis not only for one but for every decision. These principles, if closely enough related or properly unified, will make up your philosophy of life.

As we think together in this chapter concerning the levels of living, will you seek to determine the level on which you think a Christian should live and, hence, the level on which he should make his decisions?

The Instinctive Level

This is the level on which animals live. Many human activities are on this same level. A young child's behavior, for example, is largely instinctive. He has certain inborn urges or hungers that determine, to a large degree, what he does. He has the natural urge to eat, to drink, to play, and to seek ways to satisfy these and other desires.

There is nothing wrong with the natural desires or hungers of children. They may be expressed, however, in hurtful ways. While the child is immature and cannot distinguish between wise and unwise ways to express his instincts or hungers, society considers the parents primarily responsible for what he does. For example, parents who carelessly leave a bottle of poison where a child can get and drink it are generally condemned for their carelessness. The child's act is not judged to be a moral act because he did not know any better.

A part of the maturing process is to help the child to understand increasingly the proper limits within which he can express wisely his natural urges or instincts. The adult who does not recognize and stick to these proper limits is usually considered an undisciplined individual, one who is dangerous to himself and to society. This does not mean that instincts and natural urges do not continue to be important factors in a person's life. Much of the conduct, even of mature Christian men and women, is instinctively based.

Some people suggest, however, that every natural urge should be given free expression. They contend that the instinctive thing is the right thing to do. Some even go so far as to argue that if one restrains or curbs any of his natural urges, he will damage his personality. They say that a man "must be free" if he is to develop a creative personality.

Such reasoning reveals a confusion between freedom and license. One of the surest ways for a person to lose his freedom is for him to give unrestrained expression to every natural urge of his life. The most severe restriction of freedom comes from the enslavement of sin.

Man, in common with other created beings, finds his greatest freedom when he fulfils his proper function or functions. Even the powerful diesel engine that pulls the long string of freight cars has its greatest freedom by remaining on the steel rails that are made for it. Let it jump the track, and it is helpless. Similarly, man finds his greatest freedom when he fulfills the purposes for which God created him. Real freedom is living within the restraining influence of God's will.

We would consider a mother foolish and sinful if she reasoned as follows: "It is natural for my child to put anything into his mouth. I must not inhibit him. I must let him express himself freely." Wise mothers know that the child must be restrained until he can be trained to know what is proper and improper for him to eat.

As we grow older, we continue in some ways to be children. We have instincts that are right within themselves, but they may be expressed in wrong or hurtful ways. One of the evidences that we are maturing is our progressive control over these instincts, so controlling them that they find expression only in healthy ways. If expressed in such ways, they will contribute to the enrichment of our lives and to the good of others and of society.

The Customary Level

Most of what we do, we do because it is the generally accepted, the approved, the customary. It is approved by our family, our church, our community, or our crowd.

Many young people who pride themselves on their independence are frequently the most abject slaves to their particular crowd. They may be free from the control of parents and adults. They may ridicule the "mores" or customs of the community, but seldom do they assert real independence of their own age group. In defending certain lines of conduct, no expressions are more frequently used by them than the following: "Everybody is doing it," "It is expected," or "You have to _____ to be accepted by the crowd or to be popular." Such statements reveal that a person is living on the customary level, although the custom or pattern may be set by a small segment of society.

Let us admit that Christian young people should give serious consideration to what others believe to be right and wrong. They should attach particular importance to the judgment of their parents and to the position of their church. They should weigh carefully the customs and traditions of their community and the viewpoint of their gang or group.

We have not arrived, however, at the highest level of moral living if we simply accept, without thought or reflection, the customary as the final word for our lives. We are individuals who are personally responsible unto God. We should decide for ourselves what is right and wrong for us to do. Moral conduct should be based on personal thought and judgment. One may conclude that the customary standards are right, but he should not accept them simply because they are customary.

If one lived on the purely customary level, never rising above it, he would not ask the question, "Is it right; is it wrong?" Without raising any question, he would simply accept the customary as the final authority for him. However, even if people wanted to live on the customary level, society is too complicated for such a simple procedure. There are conflicts in the customs. For example, one's church may take one position, the community in general another, and other churches still another. Of course, we may make our decision entirely on the basis of our loyalty to a particular group without considering the rightness or wrongness of the custom or tradition. We have not arrived at the highest level of moral living, however, until we have thought through to a defensible Christian position.

The Conscience Level

The more intelligent people, young and old, and the ones who contribute the most to lifting the moral level of the world, are those who have thought through to clear-cut personal convictions concerning what is right and wrong for their lives. They follow their own conscience. This does not necessarily mean that they will not accept most of the traditional standards of their homes and their churches. This they may do, but they will do so because they have considered carefully these standards and have come to the conclusion that they are right or true.

Such thinking through of what is right and wrong contributes to stability of character. An individual with personal convictions will not be swept along with every wind that blows. He will not drift with the crowd. There will be times when he will have to go against the crowd, when he will have to buck the current. He will do this, knowing that only those who have the courage and strength of character to swim against the currents of life can ever change the direction of those currents.

This does not mean that Christian young people should pride themselves on being different or peculiar. Neither does it mean that they should become dogmatic, feeling that they, in a unique way or to an unusual degree, know and do the right. There is a fine but important line of distinction between depth of conviction and dogmatism. The former we should have; the latter we should avoid.

If we are wise even in regard to our own convictions, we shall retain a certain element of tentativeness. We should maintain an open mind. New insights may come to us. What we consider right today, we may consider wrong tomorrow. This will not be necessarily a sign of instability. It may be an evidence of growth.

The Christian Level

The Christian level of living is the highest level. Only when man lives on the Christian level does he become most completely man, realizing in himself the divinely ordained potential for his life. There is no necessary conflict, however, between the Christian level of living and the other levels that have been discussed.

The main difference is that the one who lives on the Christian level makes Christian principles or ideals the final test for every decision concerning what is right and wrong for his life. For example, he may accept the customs of the family, the church, and the community, but he will do so because he finds that they conform to Christian standards. One who seeks to be a real Christian and to apply the spirit and teachings of Jesus to his life may follow his conscience, but his conscience will be a Christian conscience. It will have a point of reference different from the conscience of a non-Christian. The true Christian accepts God's basic moral and spiritual principles as authoritative for his conscience.

Another important characteristic of the Christian level of living is the fact that the Christian not only has his conscience to guide him, but he has the Holy Spirit to inform and to guide his conscience. The Spirit is given to the Christian to guide him into all the truth (John 16:13). Any time he lacks wisdom he can "ask God, who gives to all men generously and without reproaching, and it will be given him" (Jas. 1:5, RSV).

The Bible and the Holy Spirit are two forces or factors in the Christian's life that the non-Christian does not have. It is true that the non-Christian can read the Bible and may receive considerable help from it. But he does not and cannot have the leadership of the Spirit in interpreting the Bible and in applying its truth to the problems and needs of his life. These two, the Bible and the Holy Spirit, should be major factors in determining for the Christian what he considers to be right and wrong. If followed sincerely, they will give to his life a tone and quality different from the non-Christian's. His life will not be conformed to the world but will be transformed or transfigured (Rom. 12:2) and will become a transforming influence in the world. He will live in the world and yet be separated spiritually from the world.

3. Christian Stewardship

An acceptance of the basic principles of Christian steward-ship will help you to decide whether or not a particular ac-tivity is right or wrong. The following are some elements in an adequate conception of Christian stewardship. Think of these in relation to some of the issues or problems discussed in Part II, such as alcohol, drugs, and dishonesty.

The Steward

The proper place to begin a study of stewardship is with the steward himself. We Christians are not our own; we have been bought with or for a price (1 Cor. 6:19–20), and that price was the death of Christ on the cross. Paul spoke of him-self as the servant or slave of Christ (Rom. 1:1; Phil. 1:1; Titus 1:1, and elsewhere). He also suggested that the only way for one to win his freedom from Satan and from the bondage of sin was for him to become the slave of Christ and of righteousness (Rom. 6:15–23).

How wonderful it is, however, that we who are slaves of Christ have been made stewards in his household. He has en-trusted his work to us. We can become co-laborers or part-ners with God in his work in the world (1 Cor. 3:9). What a privilege and responsibility it is!

As we contemplate our stewardship, let us never forget that we belong to God. He has the right to command. In his goodness he has invited us to cooperate with him in our own growth and in service to others.

Stewardship of Material Possessions

Since we belong to God, it follows inevitably that all we have belongs to him. This means that if we are thoroughly convinced that we are stewards, it will not be hard to persuade us of our stewardship of our material possessions.

Also, if all we have belongs to God, it naturally follows that we should give liberally to support the cause of Christ. We should not give less than a tithe. It is also important and normal that we should acknowledge that the remainder of our income and all of our material goods belong to God and are to be used in God-honoring ways. This aspect of stewardship relates rather directly to some of the issues discussed later, such as gambling. Included in any adequate conception of Christian stewardship is the way we make our money.

Stewardship of the Body

Since we belong to Christ, our bodies belong to him and are a part of our stewardship privilege and responsibility. Paul states it plainly for us when he says, "The body is . . . for the Lord, and the Lord for the body. . . . Do you not know that your bodies are members of Christ? . . . Do you not know that your body is a temple [tabernacle or dwelling place] of the Holy Spirit" (1 Cor. 6:13,15,19, RSV).

In the letter to the Roman church, Paul, on the basis of what he had said in the preceding eleven chapters, exhorted the Roman Christians as follows: "I appeal to you therefore, brethren, by the mercies of God, to present your bodies as a living sacrifice, holy and acceptable to God, which is your spiritual worship" (Rom. 12:1, RSV). The body can and should be holy; it can and should be acceptable unto God; it can and should be used to serve God and to bless our fellowman.

A clear understanding of the stewardship of our bodies will help us to reach wise decisions concerning the rightness or wrongness of many of the activities we face every day. We may consider the physical level a rather low basis on which to make a decision, but, whether it is low or not, many of our problems could be settled for us on that level.

One of the glorious things about Christian stewardship is the fact that things material and physical can be used for spiritual purposes. For example, the body is an absolutely essential channel or instrument if the work of the Lord is to be done in the world. This dignifies the body of the Christian.

Stewardship of Personality

The body is a phase, but only a phase, of one's personality. In one sense it would be more correct to consider the body as an instrument or channel through which one's personality finds expression in relation to others. At least personality cannot be identified with physical appearance.

By "personality" we mean to include such things as one's native mental capacity, disposition, temperament, talents, attitudes, and other things that make him a distinct individual or person. Some of these things are a part of us because of our heritage or our environment. For example, one person may be born with limited mental ability while another may be decidedly superior. They are not accountable for their much or little ability. They are responsible to God and to society for what they do with what they have. So it is with other phases of our personalities. This is a part of our total stewardship.

Stewardship of Time

This is another important phase of the stewardship life. If we belong to God—and we do if we are children of his—then we are responsible to him for what we do with the time he gives us. This does not mean that all of it is to be used in specific Christian service. Some time is required for eating and sleeping. We also know that our bodies need a certain amount of sunshine and play or recreation if they are to be in the best condition for service. Also, some recreation and social fellowship are necessary if we are to have well-balanced personalities and are to maintain healthy attitudes toward life.

A wise stewardship of time will mean that we shall avoid using any of our time for activities destructive of our own best selves, hurtful to others, or that reflect discredit on the cause of Christ.

As we mature as Christians, we shall have a deepening conviction that an increasing proportion of our time should be used for service to our fellow man and God. Sooner or later we shall awaken to the fact that what we are going to do for God and mankind must be done in a hurry. This gives to us a sense of holy urgency.

We shall guard against a waste of time. We shall continue to recognize the need for the proper amount of time for rest, relaxation, and social fellowship, but we shall consider all these as preparatory to more effective service. They will no longer be ends, of value within themselves, but means, of value because they contribute to a more effective service to God and man.

Stewardship of Influence

Here we are getting to a phase of stewardship that is somewhat more intangible but of tremendous significance. We are responsible to God for our influence. Our influence is counting for good or bad, to a lesser or a greater degree, on all we touch.

This phase of stewardship, as is true of other phases, involves both a great privilege and a great responsibility. We may not be able to preach like our pastor, sing on a par with our favorite soloist, or teach as well as the best teacher in our Sunday School, but we can live a consistent Christian life. This is one of God's best gifts, and it is available to all his children, whether they have one or ten talents. We should remember that more people are influenced for Christ by the lives of Christians than by all the sermons preached, the songs sung, or the lessons taught. We can, if we will, have a part in God's most effective way to reach people for himself.

Every child of God, regardless of how young or old, is influencing others. There is always the probability that each one of us is influencing someone else, Christian or non-Christian, more than anyone else who touches that life. How tragic if our influence leads them away from God. How wonderful if our influence is used by the Lord to lead them to himself or into a closer walk with him. Do you see the relation of this to decisions in the area of right and wrong?

Stewardship of the Gospel

Another important aspect of stewardship is the stewardship of the gospel. All other phases of stewardship find their completion and fulfilment in the trusteeship of things spiritual.

What is meant by the stewardship of the gospel? The gospel is good news. It is the good news that Jesus Christ came into the world "to seek and to save the lost" (Luke 19:10); "that everyone who believes in him may not die but have eternal life" (John 3:16); that "he is able, now and always, to save those who come to God through him" (Heb. 7:25); and the promise: "I will never turn away anyone who comes to me" (John 6:37).

This good news is committed to the children of God, to the disciples of Christ. His command is that we go, and that as we go we shall be his witnesses (Matt. 28:18–20; Acts 1:8).

We can go with the assurance that "everyone who calls on the name of the Lord will be saved." But we should remember the words that follow: "But how can they call on him, if they have not believed? And how can they believe, if they have not heard the message? And how can they hear, if the message is not preached? And how can the message be preached, if the messengers are not sent out?" (Rom. 10:13–15).

This means that some Christian stewards should go, some should help them to go, but each one has his particul responsibility for sharing the gospel with the whole world.

In addition to the preceding, each Christian steward has a direct, immediate responsibility to share the good news with those he touches from day to day. He should do this by word of mouth; but what is of equal importance, he should make known to others the good news in Christ by the life he lives before them in the classroom, on the bus, on the athletic field, in the home, as well as in the church. Our time, our talents, our influence, our bodies, our total personalities, our material possessions are all to be dedicated to making Christ a living reality in our own lives, in the lives of others, and in every area of our society.

It was Peter who admonished those to whom he was writing to be good managers of God's different gifts, or "good stewards of God's varied grace" (1 Peter 4:10, RSV). It was Paul who spoke of the "stewards of the mysteries [things hidden to the uninitiated but clear to Christians] of God" and then added, "moreover it is required of stewards that they be found trustworthy" (1 Cor. 4:1-2, RSV).

This is a big program for Christian youth. But young people are accustomed to and challenged by big programs. Christian youth must respond to the high demands of the gospel if the Christian movement is to make the impact it should on our world. If that impact is not made, it is possible that our nation, Western civilization, and even our world will collapse. In other words, our response to the challenge of Christian stewardship may be worldwide in its significance. Are we being and will we be good, trustworthy stewards?

4. The Will of God

In this book we are concerned primarily with decisions concerning right and wrong. These are moral decisions. They are moral because they affect people, including the ones making the decisions. Also, for a Christian a decision that affects the cause of Christ is a moral one.

This means, among other things, that a Christian in a time of decision should seek to honor Christ. When he has done so much for us, we should do what we can for him and for his cause. One thing we can do is to try to catch his spirit and to follow his example. He came not to do his own will but the will of the One who had sent him. He came to reveal the Father; we are to reveal him. One important way we can reveal him is by the quality of life we live for him. An expression of that quality of life is the daily decisions we make.

Others and the Will of God

We will admit that it is not always easy to know the will of God. Equally sincere people may sharply differ concerning the rightness or wrongness of some activity. Also, right in one community may be considered wrong in another. This means, at least on the surface, that right or wrong and hence the will of God, under some conditions, may be relative. There is a sense in which this is correct. An activity that is innocent or right within itself can become positively wrong·because of the attitude of people toward it. Paul's principle of eating meat offered to idols, which will be discussed in chapter 5, will apply to such situations. But let us never forget that an activity that is wrong within itself can never be made right because of the attitude of people toward it. That which is right may become wrong; that which is wrong can never become right.

This explanation may seem to contradict some things we have said previously about the individual's right and responsibility to decide for himself what is right and wrong for him to do. There may be a paradox involved but it is a very meaningful paradox. The maturing Christian should not let others dictate to him what is right; that is a personal decision. On the other hand, he should be so sensitive to the moral and spiritual well-being of others that he will let them decide, to a considerable degree, what is wrong for him to do. Even if he thinks a particular activity is entirely all right, he should not participate in it if it will be an offense or a cause of stumbling to others. This will be true because, having caught something of the spirit of his Master, he thinks primarily of others rather than of himself.

The Centrality of the Will of God

We believe that the only adequate source for or competent determinant of right and wrong for the child of God is the will of God. We believe that the right is not necessarily what man's reason dictates but what God commands. It is not what man intuits but what the divine voice says. It is not what society sanctions but what the sovereign God approves.

The most important and fundamental question that any Christian can ask when faced with a decision concerning what is right or wrong is: "What is the will of God?" This does not mean that there will be a necessary conflict between the will of God and what one's own common sense would suggest or what his home, his church, or even his group or gang would approve. It does mean that a Christian should make his decision primarily on the basis of what he considers to be the will of God. The other approaches to the right will be supplemental and will be evaluated in the light of what one interprets to be the will of God.

The Nature of the Will of God

Before we seek to answer the question "How can I know the will of God?" let us make two or three general statements concerning the nature of the will of God. (For a fuller discussion of the will of God, see T. B. Maston, *God's Will and Your Life* [Broadman Press, 1964].)

God's will is all-inclusive. It includes the major decisions discussed in Chapter 1 as well as the other decisions of life. It includes the totality of our lives. It is much broader, deeper, and more meaningful than many people think it is.

God's will is a continuing experience. Frequently, one decision is preparatory to another. If we are responsive to the leadership of the Lord, we shall have a deepening understanding of his will. This, when properly understood, will tend to give us a constant sense of tentativeness, of expectancy, of open-mindedness.

Today we may consider a particular activity in accord with the will of God for our lives. If we are obedient to him, we may discover tomorrow that he has led us to new insights, and that which we once considered right we will then understand to be wrong.

God's will is always best. His will is not only always best for him and his cause, it is also always best for us. If we are serious about doing his will, we may discover that we shall have to give up some things that we now do. There is one thing, however, about which we can be sure: what he requires us to give up is not best for us.

Since God's will is always best, we should seek to know his will; and, once knowing it, we should joyously cooperate with it. If we do this, it will seem at times that we pay dearly for our obedience. That may be true, but it will cost far more, in the long run, to fail to cooperate with the will of God. God has his martyrs, but Satan has many more. God's martyrs are joyous, singing martyrs, while Satan's martyrs are sad and sorrowful.

A missionary expressed this idea as follows: "God has so

ordered things that we cannot make a real sacrifice for him." It may and does cost something to follow Jesus, but it also "pays to serve Jesus, it pays every day, it pays every step of the way." Jesus expressed the same idea by stating what, in many ways, is the basic principle or law of life: "The man who wants to save his own life will lose it; but the man who loses his life for my sake will find it" (Matt. 16:25).

The Knowledge of the Will of God

How can we know the will of God when we are faced with a decision concerning what is right or wrong? It is not always easy. But if we sincerely want to know and are willing to do the will of God, we can and will have enough light to make the immediate decision. When other decisions have to be made, additional light will be given.

The chief tangible source for a knowledge of the will of God is the Bible. We find in the Bible a record of God's revelation or disclosure of himself to man; a self-disclosure that was climaxed in his Son who was "the exact likeness of God's own being" (Heb. 1:3). It was Jesus himself who said: "Whoever has seen me has seen the Father (John 14:9), and, "The Father and I are one" (John 10:30).

We find revealed in the Bible not only the nature and character of God but also his attitude toward and his will for man. By the latter, we do not mean that we can turn to a particular chapter and verse for an answer in every time of decision. The Bible is not a rule book. Yet, if we study it consistently, prayerfully, and obediently, we shall receive much direct and indirect help from it. The Bible is such an important factor in our knowledge of God and his will that it is safe to say that a Christian cannot know God's will as he should, in a time of decision, unless he has prepared himself for such a time by seeking through a study of God's Word to know the mind of Christ.

What can the Christian do when he cannot find a specific word in the Bible in a time of decision? He has the promise of the leadership of the Holy Spirit. One of the Spirit's functions is to teach us or to reveal to us the truth.

One way a study of the Bible helps us is to make our spiritual ears more sensitive. As we become more spiritually minded we are more able to hear "the still small voice" of the Spirit of God as he seeks to speak to us and to lead us.

It is essential if we are to know the will of God that we be willing to do it. It was Jesus who said, "Whoever is willing to do what God wants will know whether what I teach comes from God or whether I speak on my own authority" (John 7:17). After we have sincerely sought to know the will of God, there may remain an element of uncertainty. We can be assured in such times, if we are willing to do his will and start to move in the direction that we have interpreted to be the will of God, that the Lord will not permit us to go far astray. Even in the process of interpreting his will, we should keep our minds and hearts open for additional light, our faces set toward God's fuller revelation.

Responsibility for the Will of God

Some discerning young people may be saying: "All this sounds like the source of right after all is in the individual. You have come back to an individual emphasis." The latter is true, but the former does not necessarily follow.

The will of God is the final determinant of right and wrong, the ultimate source of authority for the Christian. The problem we have been dealing with in the immediately preceding paragraphs is the content of that will. We have suggested, or at least implied, that the individual has the right and the responsibility to decide for himself what the will of God is for him. He cannot shift this responsibility to someone else or to any group to which he belongs—family, friends, or church. If he is wise, he will give serious consideration to what these and others say, but the final decision is his.

No Christian concept is more basic to Protestantism in general than this idea of the responsibility of the individual. The individual Christian is to decide for himself what is right and wrong. He has direct access to God without the necessity of going through a priest or the church. This is one thing that is involved in the idea of the "priesthood of the believer."

This means that you, as you mature, will have to decide for yourself what you should do about the matters discussed in Part II. These things you should decide in the light of what you consider to be the will of God for your life.

Let us never forget, however, that the right to decide for ourselves what is the will of God for our lives involves a tremendous responsibility. We shall be held accountable by our heavenly Father and by life, as God has ordered it, for the decisions we make. This should give to each one of us a deep sense of the need for divine guidance. We should pray that our decisions will be in accord with God's holy will since we know that it will always be best for us, for those we love, for our friends, our church, our world, and for the cause of Christ.

It is wise, particularly while we are young, to seek the counsel and help of parents and other adult Christians when we are making a decision concerning the will of God in any area of our lives. We should remember, however, that the ultimate responsibility for the decision is ours, that if a mistake is made we have to pay the price.

5. Right or Wrong— Three Questions

As you approach this and the two following chapters, it will be helpful to consider their relation to the previous four. For example, chapter 1 was on decision making in general, while these chapters will suggest some specific aids in preparation for decisions related to the problems discussed in Part II. They will also suggest some simple, practical tests or ways that will help one to know the will of God and to be a good steward of his influence for God. Throughout all of our study together we need to keep in mind the level on which we as Christians should live.

It will also be helpful if you will consider these chapters (5–7) as a unit. They belong together. They merely represent different ways of approaching the same problems, of attempting to answer the same questions. There is, however, a sense in which the chapters supplement each other.

The benefit you will receive from reading these chapters, and of this entire book, will be determined largely by whether or not you sincerely want to be helped. None of us can be helped in any area of our lives, in any time of decision, unless we search honestly and fearlessly for the right with a deep determination to do what we are persuaded is right regardless of what it may be. Even God will not and cannot reveal his will to a closed mind or an unwilling heart.

Now, let us give attention to three questions that have helped many people in times of decision. These questions are applicable not only to the issues discussed in Part II but to other decisions you may face. They will be helpful not only to young Christians but to older ones as well. The latter may not have the same problems as younger people, but they have their own distinctive problems, some of which are very serious.

The Effect on Us

When we are considering whether or not we should do a certain thing, let us start on the lowest level by asking the question *"How will my participation in this activity affect me as an individual?"* This wisely can and should be followed with a series of other questions that will help us to answer more accurately the original question.

Some of the additional questions are: "How will my participation affect my body? Will it contribute to good health and to the building of a strong body, or will it tend to undermine my health and weaken my body?" The physical may seem to be a very low level on which a Christian should begin his search for what is right. In one sense it is, but there is another sense in which it is not.

The body is far more important than many of us realize. The body we have will be an asset or a liability to us all of our lives regardless of what we may do for a vocation. A healthy body is a wonderful servant or instrument; a sickly, weak body can be a terrible master. We should not participate in anything that will endanger our health or prevent the normal development and maturing of our physical selves.

Another question is, "How will my participation in this activity affect my mind, social nature, and total personality? Will participation enrich or impoverish my life?" The mental, social, and spiritual phases of our personalities are more important, in some ways, than our bodies. We have given more space to the latter primarily because that is the beginning point for our search for the right and because the physical is so frequently neglected or misinterpreted.

As Christians, we must even go beyond the consideration of the effects of our participation upon our bodies, our minds, and our moral nature. These are important but there is another phase of our total personalities that is more important. We are not merely physical bodies with minds and social natures. We are spiritual beings made in the image of God who find our highest fulfilment in fellowship with him. Our bodies, minds, and social natures should be instruments to be used by the spiritual self to promote spiritual ends. We need to ask: "How will my participation in this activity affect my spiritual life? Will it deepen or lessen my interest in things spiritual? Will it increase or decrease my sense of fellowship with my heavenly Father?"

We likewise should consider the effects of our participation on our relation to our church and on our prayer and devotional life. These things we will consider if we are serious about being real Christians instead of being just ordinary, mediocre or nominal Christians.

The Effect on Others

We admittedly started at the lowest level for the Christian. A higher level is represented by the question: *"How will my participation in this activity affect others and my influence on others?"* Other supplementary questions that might be asked are: "Is it possible that my participation may be a cause of stumbling to a weaker Christian? May it be a factor in tempting someone who is not as mature as I am? Will my participation make it easier or more difficult for me to witness to unsaved friends about Christ? Will the unsaved expect me to do this thing?" Will you agree that these and similar questions should be asked by a Christian in a time of decision?

Many times young Christians and older ones say, "I cannot see any harm in _____. I do not think it hurts me to do it." But is that the level on which a Christian should make his final decision concerning what is right for him to do? Far more important than the question "Does it or will it hurt me?" is the question "Does it or will it hurt others and my influence for good on others?"

Paul's principles regarding the eating of meat or food offered to idols provide some helpful guidance at this point

(Rom. 14:13–23; 1 Cor. 8:1–13). There are three main things that Paul said: (1) There was nothing wrong as such with eating the food or meat. (2) However, if one ate and thus sinned against the conscience of a weaker brother, he sinned against Christ. (3) Paul personally concluded that if by eating the food or meat he would cause a weaker brother to stumble, he would never eat the meat again.

This principle represents a rather strong challenge, but Christians should be willing to accept such a challenge. If Paul's principles are followed sincerely, we may discover that we will need to give up some activities that we have considered perfectly all right.

We also may find that we could participate in an activity in one community and not in another because of existing differences in attitude toward our participation. Let us emphasize, however, that the attitude of people toward what we do will not and cannot make right that which is wrong within itself. The right may become wrong, but the wrong can never become right.

It is rather important to make the preceding distinction. The attitude of people does not determine what is ultimately right; their attitude may determine whether or not a particular activity is wise or right for us in a given situation. We, as Christians, should give serious consideration to the judgment of people around us primarily because we are interested in their moral and spiritual welfare. Paul expressed it as follows: "Do not, because of food, destroy what God has done. All foods may be eaten, but it is wrong to eat anything that will cause someone else to fall into sin" (Rom. 14:20). We can substitute for the word "food" any activity concerning which we are attempting to make a decision. Man, who is God's work, or creation, is far more important than one's participation in this or that activity.

The Effect on the Cause of Christ

The highest level for a decision by a Christian is reached when he asks, *"How will my participation in this activity af-*

fect the cause of Christ?" This certainly is a very high standard. Will you not agree, however, that every Christian should be willing to ask this question and seek as best he can to answer it honestly?

A similar question that we might ask ourselves is: "Can the Lord bless and use for his glory my participation in this activity?" Paul said to the Corinthian Christians: "So whether you eat or drink, or whatever you do, do all to the glory of God. Give no offense to Jews or to Greeks or to the church of God" (1 Cor. 10:31–32, RSV).

If Paul were writing to your church or mine today, do you suppose he would put in some other words in the place of "eat" and "drink"? He related his teachings to the immediate needs and problems of people. We believe he would do the same today if he were writing to contemporary churches.

Should we not ask ourselves: "Will this activity be an occasion of stumbling or will it give offense to the church of God?" Paul suggested that the child of God, in determining what is right for him to do, should go beyond himself and even beyond other individuals and should consider the effect of his actions upon the church which is the body of Christ. Good questions for us to ask would be: "Will my participation in the activity I am considering make it more or less difficult for my church to do its work in my community and in the world? Will it reflect credit or discredit upon my church and the cause of Christ in general?"

When Christ has done so much for us, should we not be willing and even anxious to avoid anything that would be an embarrassment to him or would hurt his cause among men? The days in which we live demand unstinted devotion and selfless living. We are persuaded that many, and we hope most, Christian youth are ready to respond to that challenge.

Conclusion

The three questions that have been suggested, along with the supplementary questions, represent progressively higher levels. God has so ordered things, however, that, when properly interpreted, there can be no real conflict in the conclusions we reach on these different levels. In other words, if we make our decisions on the highest level—the effect on the cause of Christ—we shall discover that they are best not only for the cause of Christ but also for others and for ourselves. The psalmist expressed something closely akin to this idea when he said: "No good thing does the Lord withhold from those who walk uprightly" (Psalm 84:11, RSV). The Lord does not ask or expect a child of his to give up one single thing that is best for him. God may want us to give up many things, or activities that will not be best for us.

Why not try an experiment before going on to the "Three Tests" in the next chapter? On the basis of the three major questions in this chapter, decide whether or not it is right for you to participate in a particular activity. Try the questions on some activity about which you have no serious doubt. Then apply them to an activity concerning which you are somewhat doubtful.

Remember, for you to get any effective guidance from the use of the questions, you will have to want to know what is right; you will have to search sincerely for the truth.

6. Right or Wrong: Three Tests

In these chapters we are seeking to discover principles or methods by which we can know whether or not a particular activity is right or wrong. In the preceding chapter we applied the test of effect—effect upon ourselves, upon others, and upon the cause of Christ. In this chapter we are going to suggest three additional tests. Let us suggest again that you will be helped to the degree that you sincerely want to be helped and are willing to face up to the challenge presented by the tests.

The Test of Secrecy

Let us imagine that, as you read this, you are in the process of deciding whether it would be right or wrong for you to cheat. Or you might supply another activity that applies especially to you. How can the test of secrecy help you?

The following questions may help you answer the preceding question: "Are there some individuals that you would prefer not to know about it if you did that thing? What about your mother; would you be embarrassed for her to know? What about your father, your Sunday School teacher, your youth leader or counselor, your pastor, your best friend, the best Christian you know? Would you prefer for one or more of them not to know?" If you would, will you not agree that you should at least raise a question about your participation in that activity? We are not saying now that it would be right or wrong but simply that it would be questionable.

We can be sure that the truth or right is never afraid of

the light. On the other hand, wrong seeks to avoid or to hide itself from the light. It is no mere accident that most crimes are committed at night. It was Jesus who said, "And anyone who does evil things hates the light and will not come to the light, because he does not want his evil deeds to be shown up. But whoever does what is true comes to the light, in order that the light may show that he did his works in obedience to God" (John 3:20–21).

Do you remember how you reacted when you were a child and had done something that you knew your mother disapproved? Did you not evade her as much as possible? You were uncomfortable in her presence. This was true not only because you were afraid she might discover what you had done but also because there was an inner something that condemned you. You did not feel at ease in her presence.

Now, what about the activity you were considering? Will it pass the test of secrecy? Would you be willing to bring it into the full light of truth? To make the test more tangible, would it be all right with you, if you went ahead and did this thing, for that fact to be flashed on a screen at your school assembly or at a worship service in your church?

We may be able to keep our participation secret from others, but there is one who will know. God, whom we call "Our Father," will know. He sees all; he hears all; he knows all. Would we want him to know?

Test of Universality

This is another simple test that can aid us in times of decision. It will be equally helpful to young people and older people as long as they are honest seekers after truth.

We may understand this test and its significance a little better if we ask some questions. Incidentally, are you keeping in mind the activity or decision you were asked to consider at the first of the chapter? Think about it as we proceed.

One question we might profitably ask ourselves is: "Would it be all right with me if everyone else did this same thing?" Occasionally, someone in a conference where we discuss these matters answers, "Oh, sure, it would be perfectly all right." One who is inclined to answer in that way should be asked some more specific questions such as the following, which will make the general question more searching: "Would it be all right for your Mom to do it, or your Dad, or your teacher, or your pastor? Would you approve of their participation? Would you lose a little respect for them if you saw them doing it?"

What if one makes some exceptions and says: "No, I would not expect Mom to do that. I would be horrified to see my Dad doing it. I just cannot imagine my pastor participating in it." If one raises questions concerning the participation of any of these, then does not the activity fail to pass the universality test? Should not this fact raise a question concerning one's participation in it? Let us make it very personal. Is there not a considerable possibility that if we react unfavorably to the participation of another in a certain activity, someone may react in a similar way to our participation?

We should also make a general application of the universality test. Let us ask: "What kind of a family, a church, a community, a world would we have if everybody did this particular thing?" A slogan that many smaller churches used to have on their walls is applicable not only to the church but also to the family and the world. The slogan was: "What kind of a church would my church be, if every church member was just like me?"

If we admit that we would have a rather sorry family, church, community, and world if everyone did a particular thing, then, would that not mean that it would be wrong for us? If, on the other hand, we can honestly say, "We would have a better family, church, community, and world if everyone did this thing," then is it not right and wise for us to do it?

Test of Prayer

There is no higher test for any activity than to ask: "Can I pray about it? Can I ask God to go with me? Can I ask him to bless me in the doing of it?"

Should not a Christian feel free to pray about anything he does? If he does not consider it appropriate to invite the Lord to go with him or to bless him as he does that particular thing, is that not a good indication that the activity would be unwise or wrong for him?

To pass the test of prayer does not mean necessarily that we will always pray concerning that activity, but it does mean that we could, in good conscience, pray about it. We could feel perfectly at ease talking it over with our Father. Talking with him about it would be normal and natural and would create no strain in our relations.

A number of years ago Charles M. Sheldon wrote a book, which became a best seller, entitled *In His Steps*. It continues to be rather widely read. If you have not read it, we would suggest that you do so. In that book the author recommends that the Christian, at every time of decison, should ask, "What would Jesus do?" That is a good and searching question.

Some people, however, have criticized Sheldon's book and particularly his central emphasis, saying that it is an over-simplification of the problems of life. Some have suggested that a more proper and helpful question would be: "What would Jesus have *me* to do?" They contend that Jesus was God as well as man and that he lived a perfect life, which we cannot do.

There may not be as much difference in the preceding two questions as some people may think. You will remember that Paul said: "Imitate me, then, just as I imitate Christ" (1 Cor. 11:1). If Paul followed Christ—and he did—was it not natural for him to counsel the Corinthian Christians and us to follow Christ? Also, it is possible that in most, if not all, situations of life Jesus would have us do what he would do under similar circumstances. But whether we think it should be "What would Jesus do?" or "What would Jesus have me to do?" certainly we will agree that we should ask the question or questions.

You may be saying, "There is nothing that will pass such a high test. To live life on such a high level is impossible."

Surely, you do not really believe that. There are many activities that will pass the test of prayer, as well as the preceding tests.

For example, one of us played football in high school and college. He was not a Christian during the first two years of high school. His sister said that during that time he never played a game that she did not pray for him. From the time he was converted until he had finished college he never played a game that he did not first talk to the Lord about it. He asked the Lord to bless him and his teammates, to help them to play hard and clean, and to help those who were Christians, in some way, even in the midst of the game, to reveal the true Christian spirit.

There are many other activities that will pass the test of secrecy, of universality, of prayer. Also remember that if an activity will not pass the tests, it will not be best for us.

Conclusion

Have you followed through on the suggestion at the first of this chapter that you apply these tests to some particular activity? If you have not, why not try an experiment similar to the one suggested at the close of the preceding chapter? Select some activity about which you must make a decision and consistently apply the tests. See what the result will be. Do not be afraid to do it. It may be a very rewarding experience. The Lord will help you if you will ask sincerely for his guidance and wisdom.

Some may complain that the application of these tests will take the joy out of life. We believe, however, that the opposite will be true.

Christians with the deepest and most abiding joy **are those** who have a sense of the abiding presence of God. **They have a** conviction that they are within his will. Anything **that does** not pass these suggested tests will be outside of God's **will and** will sooner or later destroy the very happiness **and joy we** desire. God's good men and women, his obedient **sons and** daughters, are his happiest people.

Someone has correctly observed that most Christians have just enough religion to make them miserable. They have enough to be uncomfortable in sin; they do not have enough to keep them from sin. The only ones who ever tap the depths of the blessings that are in God are those who have the courage and the strength of character to sacrifice the lower things of life. Life on the higher levels is reserved for those who sacrifice it on the lower levels. Where do we want to live: on the mountains or high plains of vision, of challenge, and of services or in the valleys of darkness, despondency, and defeat? Right now, you may be in the process of deciding. Something that may seem to be a minor decision may set the direction of your life for the indefinite future.

Do not forget that Satan may seem to have some happy young people, but he does not have any happy old people. Is it not correct to say that even Satan's young people have a deep dissatisfaction and a hunger for a more meaningful and happier life? It will always be wise to take a deep and long look in any time of decision, however insignificant the decision may seem to be.

7. Right or Wrong— Three Sources of Light

In the last two chapters we have suggested some specific questions or tests that may help you to decide what is right or wrong when you are faced with an immediate decision. To supplement the last two chapters, we want to suggest three sources of light that are available to the Christian.

Light from Within

This chapter will be more practical and helpful if you will keep in mind some particular activity or problem. Attempt to determine whether that activity is right or wrong, wise or unwise.

One source of light in a time of decision is the light from within ourselves. God has created all of us with certain innate or inborn powers. If we are normal enough to be morally responsible, we have the power to think, to reason, to judge, to evaluate, to will. We also possess, as a part of our native equipment, a sense of oughtness or a conviction or feeling that there is such a thing as right and wrong.

God, who knows what is best for us, has put the responsibility squarely upon us to determine for ourselves what is right and wrong for us to do. It is understood that, while we are immature, this responsibility is shared by our parents, teachers, and others. The ultimate goal, however, of all moral and spiritual teaching and training is that the individual may reach full maturity. This, in turn, means that he will have the equipment with which to make wise decisions, which likewise means that he will have full responsibility for what he does.

God, who has given to man the capacity for moral living, expects man to accept the responsibilities that such capacity entails. This means that even during the maturing process, God expects us to use every inner resource we have to determine for ourselves what is right and wrong. He is not going to reveal, in some miraculous way, his will to us without our cooperation.

When faced with a particular decision, we should think through every possible angle of the problem. We should weigh, as objectively as possible, its total effects on us, on others, and on the cause of Christ. The tests, discussed in the preceding chapters, should be courageously and consistently applied: The sincere use of the resources we have will be so blessed by the Lord as to give us a sense of divine guidance that we need. The matter may be summed up as follows: When one is faced with a decision concerning right or wrong, there is no substitute for consecrated common sense.

When we have a sense of the direction in which we should go, the response to that feeling is an inner, personal one. In other words, God gives to us the power of decision. We can say yes or no to the light that comes. God will not override our wills. But we should never forget that the freedom to choose carries with it the responsibility for the choice.

Light from Without

In a time of decision we may not only receive light from within, but we may receive considerable help from without if we have eyes that see, ears that hear, minds that interpret, and wills that respond to the light that comes.

By "light from without" we mean, among other things, the aid we can receive from others, particularly those who are older, more experienced, or morally and spiritually more mature. These more mature individuals have faced similar decisions. They know, through observation and experience, the ultimate results of certain lines of conduct. They usually have the advantage of a broader perspective and a deeper insight into life and its problems than those who are more immature.

It is hoped that this will not encourage you to be too dependent upon others. As you mature—and you are in the process now—you increasingly should make up your own mind. This, in turn, does not mean that you should assert a premature independence. It does mean, however, that you should be willing to accept the responsibilities of the maturing process.

On the other hand, you should remember, regardless of how mature you may be, that you can be helped by others. No one of us has all the light he needs for many of the decisions of life. Even the light we have has come, to a considerable degree, from parents and others who have shaped our thinking and who have built into our lives basic moral ideas and ideals.

Parents, teachers, leaders, pastors, and others, who have had much more experience than you have had, woud like to save you from many mistakes. This does not mean that you should seek on every occasion of decision to talk with any one or all of them. You do not want to develop an unhealthy sense of dependence on others. You do not want to become a "counselor addict"; one who seeks counsel from every counselor who comes along.

Much of the soundest counsel you will receive from parents, teachers, leaders, pastors, and other adults, will come as you listen to them in the home, the classrooms, or the church. Some of it will come through formal instruction; much of it will be gathered from casual conversation.

This does not mean that you should not seek help of parents and adult friends when you really need it. This you can and should do, admitting frankly your limitations and your need for additional light. You will seek counsel from a particular individual because you believe he is more mature than you are. You go to him also because you have confidence in his basic integrity and his genuine interest in you.

As a result of your confidence in the one from whom you seek advice, you certainly will give serious consideration to any light you receive from him. This should be true, in particular, of the counsel received from parents. Parents, with rare exceptions, are more interested in you and in your welfare than anyone else. They would like to use the light that has come to them, as they have traveled life's pathway, to light your pathway and to save you from some of the errors they have made along the way.

You may be disappointed at times that the adults from whom you seek advice do not give you more positive guidance. In most cases this is done deliberately. The wise counselor hopes to lead you to make your own decision with as little suggestion or direction from him as necessary. He wants to shed the light that will help you to see the way you should go. He wants you to discover for yourself as much of that light as possible. He then hopes that you will make your own decision. If he can succeed in leading you to such a personal decision, he knows that it will be more meaningful to you than a decision you make at his suggestion.

There are also individuals whom you have never met who may be helpful to you in times of decision. They are the authors of articles, pamphlets, and books. Some of these may be found in your church or community library.

There is still another source of light from without that would save many young people from tragic mistakes if they would keep their eyes and ears open and their minds alert. The light we are referring to is that which comes by observing, in the lives of others, the ultimate results of particular lines of conduct.

For example, if you are trying to decide whether it is right or wrong for you to use drugs, to drink, to have sex relations, observe the results in the lives of those who participate in such activities. Watch for the more immediate as well as the final results. What about some of your acquaintances: did you notice any good or bad effects on them when they began to participate in one or more of these activities? What about the effects on their personalities? What about their appreciation for the finer things of life? What seemed to be the effect on their relation to their church and the Lord?

If you are to see the full picture, however, and hence to

judge the results fairly, you must look beyond the high school or the college campus. You should even study the influence of one's participation in a particular activity on the home and on society in general. You should visit the slums and jails of your city or community.

On one such visit, the police captain said that he was sure the police department had arrested "Aunt Mary" at least 700 times for drunkenness. He reported that there was a time when she was a highly respected woman in the community. She had become a slave to drink, as is true of millions of other men and women. What a contrast between "Aunt Mary" and the beautiful advertisements for alcohol in the magazines and the attractive posters on the billboards. "Aunt Mary" would considerably mar those pictures, but she belongs in them if they are going to be accurate. Young people need to see "Aunt Mary" in those pictures. If they did, she would help them to know what to do about drinking.

This is merely one illustration of what is meant by the light from without. Intelligent observation will save us from many mistakes.

Light from Above

This is another source of light, available to all children of God. We can and should utilize it in times of decision. Let us suggest again that the Lord expects us to use the resources we have to choose the right and to refuse the wrong. This is different, however, from saying that we have, within ourselves, all the resources we need for life's decisions. An important step in any wise decision concerning a major problem is a proper sense of our own limitations. We should acknowledge that we cannot think as clearly as we should unless we have the leadership of the Holy Spirit. We should admit our need for the Lord's guidance and should seek that guidance even as we use every resource available to us in an attempt to determine what is right or wrong.

This means that as you ask the questions, as you make the tests suggested in preceding chapters, you should do so in the spirit of prayer. Also, as you seek the counsel and advice of others, you should ask the Spirit of God to lead them and you.

Even when you have sought prayerfully all the light possible from within and from without, you may still be in doubt. At such times, call to mind what James says: "But if any of you lacks wisdom, he should pray to God, who will give it to him; for God gives generously and graciously to all" (Jas. 1:5).

An important source for the light that comes from above is the Bible. The Bible is not a rule book, but wherever it speaks specifically it is authoritative. The Bible contains basic principles that will provide the foundation for wise Christian choices. If we saturate ourselves in its spirit and build its ideals into our lives, we shall have the moral and spiritual alertness that is needed to choose wisely.

In response to your prayers, your Bible study, and your sincere seeking, God may not flood your soul with light, but he will give you enough light to take the next step. Follow whatever light you have, although it may not be more than a gleam, with complete confidence that God will give you additional light as it is needed. This will be true in regard to the issues we are going to discuss in Part II. It also can be and will be true, if you will do your part, in regard to other decisions you shall make as you journey life's pathway.

8. Principles and Practice

The preceding chapters of Part I have dealt with principles of Christian conduct. They have been written with the hope and prayer that they will be helpful to you. We trust you have not bypassed those chapters. If you accept the principles, apply them honestly, and utilize the sources of help suggested, you can be trusted, to a large degree, to decide for yourself what is right or wrong for you to do.

In the chapters in Part II we shall attempt to apply those general principles to some of the more important issues among young people. Naturally, we cannot review all the pertinent principles in connection with each problem. It is hoped that you will study these chapters deliberately and slowly enough to review and to apply the basic principles, including the questions and tests suggested.

A Review of the Principles

Before we proceed to a discussion of specific problems, it may be of some value to review some of the more significant conclusions or principles of Part I. They are as follows:

1. To live is to make decisions (chapter 1).

2. While all of us live, to a certain degree, on the instinctive, the customary, and the conscience levels, the level on which a Christian should live is the distinctly Christian level (chapter 2).

3. The Christian is not his own. He—his body, his mind, his total personality—belongs to God, but God has seen fit to make him a steward. Being a steward, all he has of material

goods, of time, and of talents belongs to God and is to be used under the direction of God to serve God and his fellow man (chapter 3).

4. The final source of authority for man is not within himself or within the social group or community to which he belongs, but it is the will of God, which man can know and which he will discover is always best for him (chapter 4).

5. When we are faced with a decision involving right or wrong, we can find help by asking three questions: how will my participation in this activity affect me? others? the cause or Christ? (chapter 5); by making three simple tests: the test of secrecy, the test of universality, and the test of prayer (chapter 6); and by utilizing three sources of light: the light from within, the light from without, and the light from above (chapter 7). These questions, these tests, these sources of light are not only methods by which we can know the right and the wrong, but they also contain some fundamental principles that we can use in making our decisions.

Importance of the Principles

As you have read the chapters and as you have reviewed the principles, have you thought through and understood them? A more important question is: "Do you accept them as valid for a Christian?"

Whether or not you agree with the principles outlined in the preceding chapters, it is very important for you to have a core of Christian principles which will provide you with a base of operation. Before long, if not at the present time, you are going to be on your own. Every decision will be yours to make. An essential part of the preparation is the formulation of a Christian philosophy of life, a philosophy that is built upon sound Christian principles.

Certainly, we would like to think that you will agree with us concerning the problems we shall discuss in Part II. Likely that will not be true. Let us say frankly that we are much more interested in your acceptance of the basic principles of Part I. Our viewpoint is that if you have a sound basis for the decisions of life and honestly search for the right, then as you mature you will finally, if not immediately, arrive at the right position concerning most if not all of the problems and decisions you will face.

One of our chief concerns is that you will think carefully through every problem or decision. We would rather for you to think and disagree with us than to agree and not think.

Our main concern, however, is that you be honest in your search for what is right and wrong. We know if that is true, then God will give you guidance and assurance and will not permit you to go very far astray. The searching mind and the willing heart will know what is right and wrong.

This searching is a lifetime job. It will be most unfortunate if you conclude that you have all the knowledge and light you need concerning any of the problems of life. God himself cannot lead a closed mind. He reveals additional light to those who set their faces toward the open road. Principles may be fixed and secure; an understanding and the application of them is a continuing process.

Change in Approach

In Part II which deals with specific areas of decision, we have found it advisable to change our approach to some degree. You will find a more frequent use of questions and less often a statement of a positive position, although we will not hesitate to make the latter when it seems wise or necessary to do so.

This change in approach and emphasis has been made deliberately. One reason for the change is that we want you to apply for yourself the basic principles to the specific problems considered. We want you to answer for yourself the question: "Is this activity right or wrong for me as a Christian?" We do not think you will have much difficulty knowing our position. But it is far more important for you to be led to make a wise, personal decision than for you to understand or to agree with our position.

In the chapters in Part II we try to provide you with the

facts needed to make a wise decision. In some cases questions are provided to help guide you in relating the principles in Part I to these facts. Not all important issues are included. These are examples of some of the more common issues which young people face. If other problems are more urgent to you, the same basic approach can be used in dealing with them: (1) get the facts, (2) apply Christian principles, (3) make your decision.

If you think through to a clear-cut, defensible Christian position on any problem, you must take time to deliberate, to meditate, and to pray. It is hoped that you will be willing to give whatever time is necessary. There is a possibility that a decision concerning your relation to one of these activities may be the most important decision you face at this particular time. A right decision in regard to that problem may provide the basis for many other wise decisions in the years to come.

Do not forget that *we* once faced the same decisions that many of you are in the process of making. Also, through the years we have been interested in young people and have given much time to personal and group conferences with them concerning these problems. Try, as best you can, to think of these chapters as personal chats with you or as conferences with a group of Christian youth.

Part II: Issues

9. Marijuana

Sharon was pretty and popular. She laughed a lot and ran around with the "in" group at school. One night someone brought some marijuana cigarettes to a party. At first Sharon refused to smoke one. But her friends kept urging her to "blow a stick." Finally she gave in. A boy taught her how to inhale and hold the smoke. Sharon had come to the party worried about her studies and upset over an argument with her mother. As she began to get high, her troubles seemed to fade. After the party the "in" group began to smoke marijuana regularly, and Sharon went along. Her life revolved more and more around the drug. Now she is beginning to prefer a marijuana high to normal life. Her grades are falling, sometimes she steals to buy a joint, and apart from the grass group, she has few friends.

A Big Issue

The use of marijuana is definitely a big issue. In recent years its use has grown rapidly, mainly among young people. No one knows how many people use marijuana. Since it is illegal to sell or possess it, buying, selling, and using it goes on without records being kept. The extent of use seems to vary greatly from place to place. In some high schools and colleges the majority of students apparently have experimented with pot. In others very few have. Marijuana is increasingly common among elementary and middle schoolers too. Several young people felt pot was such a big problem that we should give a separate chapter to it. So we have.

Marijuana—known also as "grass," "pot," "Mary Jane," "Acapulco Gold," "weed," "hay," "boo," and "tea"—is widely used. Students, soldiers, working young adults, and hippies consume approximately 300 tons of marijuana a year in this country. The amount has been increasing annually. In one college estimated use of pot went from 20 percent of the students to 70 percent during a three-year period. In a number of high schools it is estimated that 30 to 50 percent of the students have used marijuana.

Marijuana is also an important issue because it is a rallying point for youth against the adult establishment. The fact that marijuana—the youth drug—is illegal while alcohol—the adult drug—is legal angers many young people. They feel that they are being discriminated against. Groups have been formed to work to legalize marijuana. Part of the plan seems to be to get such a widespread use of grass that legalization will be forced.

Another argument for legalization is that alcohol is legal and that marijuana is no more dangerous than alcohol. But do two wrongs make a right? Shouldn't this line of reasoning really lead to stricter control of alcohol rather than looser laws for marijuana?

Pressures to Smoke Pot

Marijuana is available on a large scale. Much of it is imported from Mexico. Some is grown in the United States. Marijuana is prepared from a plant, *cannabis sativa L.*, which is hearty and grows almost anywhere in a temperate climate. Pot is available in a number of forms and strengths. It can be smoked, eaten, or drunk. The ease of growth, volume of production, and variety of forms make marijuana widely available.

Why do so many young people use pot? The reasons differ from person to person. But a number of common factors seem to be involved.

Openness to pot among young people is due in part to the widespread use of drugs in our society. To take a pill for pains and worries is a way of life for many Americans. Millions use drugs both to go to sleep and to wake up. Alcohol and cigarettes are an everyday part of life for the majority of adults. It is not surprising that young people see little or nothing wrong with using marijuana. Drug abuse by adults does not make pot right for young people. But it does help explain why many youth have so little resistance to drug use.

Many young people smoke pot because of the pressure of other youth. Not wanting to be left out, they go along when the group they are with uses marijuana. They smoke pot because it is the in thing to do. This is how Sharon got started.

Some try grass out of rebellion against adult society in general and parents in particular. A few, knowing how most adults react against marijuana, smoke pot simply to irritate adults.

A number try marijuana just to see what it is like, to experiment. They have been told about the pleasure and heightened sensations which pot smoking brings. This sounds appealing so they try marijuana.

Do you know young people who smoke pot for any of these reasons? Have you felt any of these pressures? Are other pressures to try marijuana even stronger in your school and community?

Once a person tries marijuana he may continue to use it. Persons with personality defects are particularly prone to keep on smoking pot. The people who continue find that the drug meets some need. Some enjoy the sensation which comes with smoking it. It may relieve frustration, release tension, relax the mind, increase sociability, or ease a feeling of inferiority.

If a person becomes dependent on the drug, he usually defends its use. Many arguments are used to defend smoking pot. If you live in an area where Acapulco Gold is common, you have probably heard most of these arguments: Marijuana is not addicting. It is not harmful when used in moderation. It helps you relax. It is not dangerous. It is not as bad as alcohol. Everybody uses drugs. Smoking pot is a purely private act. A look at the facts will help you evaluate such claims.

The Facts About Marijuana

The facts about marijuana are not all in. Research and experiments on its effect are under way. Some things are known for certain about pot; others seem to be true.

The effect of marijuana varies greatly. It depends primarily upon the strength of the dosage and the personality of the user. One of the frightening things about pot is that the strength of the dosage is seldom known; there is no control on purity or potency. Further, no one is able to tell in advance how it will affect him. Some people experience little effect from a mild dose while others may have a severe reaction. Sometimes a single marijuana cigarette triggers a serious mental problem.

The first reaction to marijuana is usually mild intoxication. Dizziness, sluggishness, time and space distortion, and muddled thinking follow. In many cases hallucinations, anxiety, and hysteria go along with the intoxication. Extreme mental and emotional disturbances are a rare but dangerous possibility. In some people marijuana seems to play a key role in personality changes.

Physically the effect of pot is uncertain. There is some evidence that marijuana may damage the brain. Most research indicates that there is no addiction; that is, the body does not develop a physical need for marijuana. But its use does lead to psychological dependence which is sometimes more difficult to correct than physical addiction. When a person is dependent on grass, a weed controls his life. Doesn't it seem degrading to let a weed take over the life of a human being?

The majority of users of so-called hard drugs, such as heroin, at one time smoked pot. Certainly not everyone who tries marijuana becomes a narcotic addict. But there is a link between marijuana and other drugs. As a youth gets involved in the drug culture he is tempted, and sometimes pressured, into trying stronger and stronger stuff. Many resist this pressure. Others do not and get hooked into the horror of narcotic addiction. No one sets out to become a junkie. Most persons feel that they can control their drug habit. But no one knows in advance whether he can resist the pull into increased drug use.

According to the law, possessing marijuana is a major crime. Anyone who possesses pot runs the risk of a heavy jail sentence and a prison record. Such a record can blight your entire life. You may feel that the law is too severe. Whether it is or not makes little difference once you have been arrested, tried, and convicted. You are marked for life.

The impact of marijuana on society is difficult to measure. Harm results from grass, but how much is anyone's guess. Many parents have been deeply hurt by children who smoke pot. Persons have been killed and injured in automobile accidents caused by the mental confusion of a marijuana user. Vast sums of money are spent enforcing laws against marijuana when the funds are desperately needed in other ways. Hospital and other medical resources are tied up helping pot users who have had a bad reaction. Some persons steal to get money to buy grass. The total cost in lives and money of supporting Mary Jane is terribly high.

Toward a Decision

Like Sharon, you may face strong pressure to try pot. If not, you likely will. Don't you believe it would be helpful to make up your mind about marijuana while not under the immediate pressure of a group? Here are some questions to consider as you decide what to do about marijuana:

What level of living are you on now in regard to marijuana —the instinctive, customary, conscience, or Christian? What do you believe the Christian level calls for concerning marijuana?

Which would best express Christian stewardship—using marijuana or leaving it alone?

What do you genuinely believe is God's will about the use of pot?

In light of the facts about marijuana, do you think using or refusing it is best for your body? your mind? your future?

How do you feel you can best express love for your parents

in regard to grass? If you are angry with your parents and want to hurt them, do you really think using marijuana is worth the cost to you?

Who should you believe about the effect of pot—the user, whose self-interest is served in getting you involved or the nonuser, who has an unselfish interest in you?

Considering the effect on others and on society by marijuana, how do you feel you can best show love to others and build a better world—by saying yes or no to pot?

10. Alcohol

The majority of Americans drink. And many young people go along with the masses. They live on the customary level. But a large number of young people resist the urging, "Come on. Have a drink. What's the matter? Scared?" They say, "No thanks." To drink or not to drink is a question you probably already face. If not, you will likely be forced to deal with it soon. Here are some things to keep in mind as you make your choice.

The Pressure to Drink

The pressure to drink is great. From every side a young person is urged to join the drinking crowd. Even though it is illegal to sell alcoholic beverages to minors, most youth know where they can readily get beer, wine, or whiskey. In some homes parents make alcohol available to their children. Persons who drink often urge others to follow their example. In fact, a drinker frequently gets irritated with someone who resists his urge to "have a drink." Advertising, movies, and television all picture drinking as glamorous and sophisticated.

In addition to pressures from without there are pressures from within. The desire to go along with the crowd, to not be left out, is strong. When you are with a group and most are drinking it is not easy to refuse to join in. Drinking is often thought of as an adult practice and many youth begin to drink in an effort to be adult. On the other hand, some drink in reaction to their parents or culture. Wanting to break free from home restrictions, a young person may begin to drink because his parents forbid him to. The desire to experiment, to try something new, is strong in most young people. A number of persons take their first drink just to see what it is like.

For many people, drinking itself produces a craving to drink more. These persons are usually insecure and need a crutch to help them meet special demands. They learn that alcohol eases anxiety, calms fears, and makes them feel more confident. Or they discover that drinking eases their hurt over defeat, shortcomings, or failure. Alcohol can cause a person to forget his troubles and escape his problems—for a while. So the weak, insecure, or emotionally disturbed individual often has a strong yearning for alcohol because he has discovered what it does for him. Many of these become alcoholics.

If you drink, honestly face up to the reasons why. Try to pinpoint the pressures on you to drink and see which ones you have given in to. If you don't drink, which pressures seem strongest pushing you to begin? Think of ten persons you know who drink and try to determine why they do.

Defenses for Drinking

Part of the pressure to drink comes in the form of the many defenses made for drinking. Few defend drunkenness, but many argue for moderation. They insist that moderate drinking hurts no one and may be beneficial. One problem with this argument is that moderate drinking frequently leads to immoderate drinking and alcoholism. Over six million Americans are alcoholics. None of them started drinking to become an alcoholic. All of them intended to be moderate and felt that they could control their drinking. But they were wrong. No one knows whether or not he has the personality weaknesses that may cause him to be an alcoholic.

Some argue that drinking can be beneficial. They point out that alcohol eases tension and soothes jangled nerves. A few even claim that one drink might improve a tense person's driving. Many use alcohol as a form of medicine for some diseases. In an ancient age, prior to modern medical science, such claims for alcohol might have justified its use. But with modern tranquilizers and medicines, does it really make sense to turn to alcohol for medical reasons?

Young people sometimes defend their drinking on the ground that most adults drink, including many famous, successful persons. Many adults do things, however, which sensitive youths reject—pollute the air, foul the water, fail in marriages, and act irresponsibly as citizens. Mature young people don't do things simply because adults do them. A growing number of youth are evidently more discerning and responsible than many adults.

It is argued by a few that drinking alcohol is less harmful than taking other drugs, such as heroin. But does being less harmful make it right? This argument would lead you to say that anything other than the worst of acts is all right. Burning down a man's house is less harmful than cutting off both his arms, but does this make it right?

Some defend alcohol on the basis of the Bible. They claim that the Bible does not condemn drinking, only drunkenness. They point out that Jesus drank, Paul recommended wine to Timothy, and the Old Testament contains praise for wine. In order to apply the Bible's statements about alcoholic beverage to us today several facts need to be understood.

For one thing, distilled alcoholic beverages with high alcoholic content—like whiskey—were not known in Bible times. Wine, made from fermented grapes, was used in the Bible period. It was lower in alcoholic content than most of today's hard liquor. In the ancient world water was often unsafe to drink; fermented grape juice was sometimes safer. In modern America safe water is available to drink. Also, wine and oil were an important part of primitive medicine; we have far better medicines today. People in Bible times were not subjected to high-powered advertising nor to the pressure of modern, urban life—both of which contribute to heavy drinking and alcoholism. In short, persons living in the period when the Bible was written faced a situation in regard to alcohol far different from that people face today.

Problems with Drinking

Alcohol hurts the person who drinks it. Even in small doses alcohol harms body and mind. Evidence continues to pile up about the damage done to human cells by alcohol. Brain cells are killed, for example; and brain cells are never replaced. Alcohol also damages the stomach, intestines, liver, kidneys, and other vital organs. All other things being equal, the health of a drinker is not as good as that of a nondrinker. The life expectancy of the drinker is less than that of the nondrinker. That is why some insurance companies offer lower rates to nondrinkers.

Alcohol quickly affects the part of the brain which controls emotion, speech, and reason. In a sense alcohol tends to reduce the drinker from the human to the animal level of existence. The more a person drinks the more he loses control of himself. The exact way in which he acts under the influence of alcohol will depend largely on his personality.

Alcohol removes inhibitions. People who drink often do and say things which they later regret. They may hurt someone's feelings or insult them. A boy who is normally peaceful may under the influence of alcohol become obnoxious and start a fight. Or a girl who drinks may let a boy do things to her sexually that she would not let him do under normal circumstances.

Accidents in the home, at work, and in travel are often due to alcohol. Alcohol and automobiles when mixed result in about 30,000 deaths and in over a million injuries each year. Drinking and driving don't mix. The saying "If you drive don't drink, if you drink don't drive" is on target. You don't have to be drunk to be dangerous behind the wheel of a car. A small amount of alcohol slows reflexes and increases the possibility of an accident. Approximately half of the fatal automobile accidents involve drinking drivers. Wouldn't it be terrible to have to live with the fact that you killed someone because you were driving under the influence of alcohol?

Society in general suffers because of alcohol. Police and jail costs are increased by those who drink. Approximately 50 percent of all police man hours are spent dealing with alcohol-related offenses. Insurance rates are high partly because of the unnecessary damage to life and property caused by drinking drivers. Businesses suffer loss due to alcohol; drinking employees are inefficient and many miss work because of their drinking. Work-related losses due to alcohol total more than $7 *billion* a year. Alcohol also increases health and welfare costs. Don't you feel that we could have a better world if the billions of dollars which alcohol costs each year were spent on constructive purposes?

Wherever alcohol goes it leaves a trail of tears . . . a little boy sobbing because his daddy was killed by a drinking driver, an unmarried girl weeping because she is pregnant, a young man ashamed because his mother is an alcoholic, a family in poverty because the husband spends so much for alcohol that they can't pay their bills, a man fired because he couldn't control his drinking, a student horribly disfigured from a drunken brawl.

An Approach to Decision

How can a Christian know what to do about alcohol? The principles set forth in Part I can supply help as you make up your mind. For example, read chapter 3 and apply the ideas of stewardship of body and mind to alcohol. Chapter 5 is also very clear. relate the three questions discussed there to alcohol. Will alcohol hurt or help you? Others? The cause of Christ?

Although the Bible may not provide specific instructions about alcohol, it does set forth helpful guidelines. For example, one of the clearest teachings in the Bible is that we are to love God with all of our being and our neighbor as ourselves. What does such love call for in regard to alcohol? The facts about drinking can help answer this question.

Can you best love God by drinking or not drinking? Remember, alcohol disrupts relations with other persons, including God who is a person. It makes the drinker less efficient. It cuts down on mental ability. It slows physical reaction. Do you think that God will be pleased if you give him a second-rate you? Does it honor God when we abuse our minds and bodies?

Can you love your neighbor better by drinking or not drinking? Remember that people who drink are more likely to destroy the lives of others. Persons who use alcohol run the risk of injuring another in an accident. Supporting the use of alcohol increases social problems, ups the tax bill, raises insurance rates, and hurts business. Even the person who drinks alone and in moderation contributes to the spread of alcohol. And the person who himself is able to keep his drinking under control may lead someone to begin to use alcohol who cannot control his drinking and will become an alcoholic. Are these ways to show love for others?

In light of God's purpose for your life and the facts about alcohol, what do you feel you should do about drinking? What do you feel the Christian level of living calls for?

11. Other Drugs

Diane was a beautiful, bright, popular young lady. She came from a happy home. Her dad made good money. She had an apartment of her own and a promising future. The pressure to experiment with drugs was great, however, and she began to take LSD. The flashbacks became uncontrollable. She told her brother she thought she had blown her mind. The drug experiment ended by Diane jumping to her death—a suicide.

Jimmy was a scrawny little boy from the slums. His family was poor. The place where he lived was filthy and overrun with rats. Noise and violence filled his days. Most of the people he knew were on drugs. So he began to take them too. Soon he was shooting heroin. One day Jimmy was found dead . . . an overdose. He was twelve years old.

Young people from wealthy and poor families, from pre-teens to early twenties, from good homes and bad, in inner city ghettos and in suburbs are caught up in drug use. The largest number come from the cities. But rural areas are not without drug abusers. A few of the young people involved know what they are getting into. Most do not. What begins as a fun spree often ends in tragedy.

Some are tricked into getting hooked on drugs by someone who slips a drug into their food or drink. Many pushers—those who sell drugs—will do almost anything to increase the number of persons on drugs. They will lie and resort to trickery and violence.

Do you know about the different kinds of drugs available today? Do you know their source? What they do to people?

What you can expect if you get involved? This chapter may help you deal with the drug problem by providing guidance in answering questions such as these.

A drug is a chemical compound capable of producing a physical, emotional, or mental change in a person. Drugs serve mankind in many ways. In the hands of a competent doctor they may be useful for treating physical, mental, and emotional illness. But they can be abused. Drug abuse occurs when drugs are taken for no sound medical or scientific purpose. There are several different types of drugs which are often abused.

Solvent Sniffing

A weird variety of material has been used by young people to bring about abnormal mental and emotional reactions. For example, youth have tried sniffing glue, paint thinner, lacquer, and gasoline. All these items are easy to obtain and inexpensive. Most users consider them safe. But safe they are not.

The early effect of solvent sniffing is a giddy, silly, mildly intoxicated feeling. If the sniffing continues the person involved develops slurred speech, double vision, drowsiness, and lack of coordination. Unconsciousness, coma, and death can result. Under the influence of solvent sniffing some persons have committed violent acts.

Repeated sniffing of solvents can result in physical harm. One physician listed as possible results damage to the kidneys, liver, brain, and bone marrow. The latter can result in aplastic anemia, a fatal blood disease. Solvent sniffers are also prime targets for drug pushers who promise even greater kicks.

Hallucinogens

Hallucinogens, or the so-called mind-bending drugs, have attracted much attention. Marijuana is actually in this class although it is covered in the Federal narcotic laws. It has been treated in a separate chapter. Included in this group are d-lysergic acid diethylamide (LSD), peyote, psilocybin, mescaline. and dimethyltryptamine (DMT).

The most widely abused of the hallucinogens is LSD, better known as acid. It is colorless, odorless, and tasteless. Minute amounts (1/280,000 of an ounce) are capable of extreme effects. LSD is taken in several ways: deposited on sugar cubes, put in cookies or crackers, or swallowed in pill form.

The effects of LSD vary with the drug dosage and the user's personality. Basically the drug affects the central nervous system producing changes in mood and behavior. The user takes a "trip" usually lasting from four to twelve hours, but it may last for days. Experiences on the "trip" differ from individual to individual but these are common: Senses appear sharpened and brightened. Sounds are felt and colors tasted. Fixed objects seem to breathe. Bodies, including the LSD user's, appear weird and oddly shaped. Fear and a sense of isolation are strong.

The effects of LSD on the user after the "trip" vary widely. Some suffer long-lasting mental disorder. Many act out personality defects in exaggerated ways. A number attempt suicide. In some persons latent mental illness is activated. One of the most terrifying characteristics of LSD is that a "trip" can begin weeks or even months later without the drug being taken again; the user literally loses control of his mind.

There is also evidence of damage to chromosome structure; this can result in birth defects in children of parents who have used LSD. No one knows for sure what the long-term effects will be. As one doctor said, "Medically unsupervised use of LSD is analogous to playing chemical Russian roulette."

Amphetamines and Other Stimulants

Another group of drugs directly stimulates the central nervous system. The most widely used stimulant in the United States is caffein, an ingredient in coffee, tea, cola, and other beverages. Cocaine, controlled under the Federal narcotic law, is another member of this group. Amphetamines—better known as pep pills, bennies, dexies, eye openers, and copilots— are the most seriously abused drugs in this category.

Amphetamines produce alertness, an ability to go without

sleep for long periods, and increased activity. No physical dependence results. But tolerance develops and increased quantities of the drug can cause bizarre effects. An overdose often results in wild speech, profuse sweating, and shakiness. Sometimes serious mental disorder occurs. The person may feel persecuted, or that he is covered with horrible insects.

An abused drug chemically related to amphetamine is methamphetamine—known popularly as speed, crystal, or meth. Users rapidly develop a tolerance which leads to dangerous doses. The hippie community quickly learned that "speed kills" and backed away from its use.

Some young people take pep pills to help them study for long periods or drive great distances without getting sleepy. Driving while taking pep pills can be dangerous. Many wrecks are caused by drivers on amphetamines. People who seriously abuse these drugs sometimes commit violent acts and crimes under their influence.

Barbiturates and Other Sedatives

Another branch of the drug family includes sedatives and tranquilizers. Alcohol, discussed in a previous chapter, is part of this group and causes more problems than any other drug. The next most abused drugs in this group are the barbiturates, known by many slang terms such as "barbs," "sleeping pills," "candy," and "goofballs." Barbiturates have many legitimate medical uses. But they are also often abused.

Abuse of barbiturates results in slurred speech, staggering, and quick temper. Under influence of the drug a person may become emotionally erratic and suffer delirium, hallucinations, and impaired judgment. Overdose results in death. Many people have accidently killed themselves by mixing alcohol and barbiturates. Since both are depressants a death dealing dose can be taken without the victim being aware of the danger.

Tolerance develops with barbiturates and more and more of the drug is required to gain the same effect. Under heavy usage physical dependence develops. Withdrawal can be very dangerous and sometimes causes death.

A person on goofballs is a threat not only to himself but to other people as well. Although violent assault is sometimes blamed on abuse of barbiturates, the most common problem is automobile accidents. A drug abuser made drowsy by goofballs is a dangerous driver.

Narcotics

Some people speak of all drugs as narcotics. But actually, narcotics form only one branch of the drug family. A narcotic is a drug which produces a stupor. It is a depressant. True narcotics include morphine, codeine, heroin, paregoric, meperidine, and methadone. Federal narcotic laws include under the term narcotic the drugs cocaine and marijuana, neither of which is a true narcotic. Both are potentially dangerous drugs, however.

Of the true narcotics the most frequently used for non-medical purposes is heroin. This whitish powder is taken through the mouth, nose, or veins. It produces a number of effects: apathy, drowsiness, diminished sex and hunger drives, impaired mental and physical activity. Repeated use of heroin results in physical dependence. Also, a person needs larger and larger doses to produce the same result.

Once a person is hooked he is desperate for money to buy drugs. If he can't get a fix (a dose of the drug) he goes into withdrawal. In withdrawal the addict goes through terrible pain—burning eyes, hot and cold flashes, cramps, crawling flesh, diarrhea, and inability to sleep. The pain lasts for days and is usually followed by severe depression. Medical help can ease some of the pain in withdrawal but it is still a terrible experience.

With a fix the addict avoids the horror of withdrawal. But the more the addict shoots heroin into his body the more it destroys him. Heroin kills. For some, death comes suddenly in an overdose. For others, their fate is living death. Although the initial sensation of the drug may be pleasant, the long-range effect will be pain and suffering.

Time and again the addicts puncture their flesh to inject

the drug. Lack of sanitation often leads to horrible sores and ulcers at the puncture points. Within their bodies heroin takes away appetite; malnutrition results and health sags. Sexual desire fades. Heroin robs them of interest in other people, and they become extremely selfish. Heroin short-circuits the cough reflex and the addict's lungs tend to fill with mucus. Lack of sensitivity to pain can lead to burned flesh, infection, and serious bruises. Constipation is a constant problem. It is not surprising that few narcotic addicts live to old age.

Heroin is an illegal drug. It cannot be lawfully imported or manufactured. Organized crime is closely linked to heroin. Members of organized crime are responsible for importing and wholesaling most of the heroin available in the United States. The profit is immense; high prices are charged for the drug. An addict may spend $100 a day to support his habit. Since many are unable to keep a good job they often steal to secure funds to buy fixes. Women sometimes support their habit through prostitution. Narcotics are linked with unlawful activity in many different ways.

In Light of the Facts

In light of the facts, what will you do about the use of drugs? The pressures to use the drugs described in this chapter are much like those related to alcohol, marijuana, and tobacco. Most of them are easily obtained. Other young people use them and will encourage you to use them too. A desire to be liked, to experiment with something new, to rebel against adult authority may push you to try the drugs.

A number of arguments are made in defense of drug use, such as: "Don't knock it if you haven't tried it." "You haven't lived until you've tried it." "Adults are lying when they talk about the dangers of drugs." "Everybody uses drugs today in one way or another." "Using drugs is a personal matter and no one's business but yours." What weaknesses do you see in each of these arguments?

The pressure is on to use drugs. In making a responsible, Christian decision perhaps these questions will help you:

Will using drugs help or harm me physically? mentally? emotionally? spiritually?

Will using drugs cause me to help or harm my parents? friends? people I don't even know?

Will using drugs help or hinder me in an effort to make a better world? In developing my talents and abilities? In my vocation? In my family life?

In light of the facts, are the reasons given for using drugs really valid?

Do the biblical guidelines of love for God, love for neighbor, and love for self point toward using or avoiding drugs?

12. Tobacco

One-half of the nation's teen-agers are steady smokers by the time they are eighteen years old, according to the director of the Public Health Service's National Clearing House for Smoking and Health. Tobacco certainly seems to be a big issue for young people.

Much has been said about tobacco recently. Since cigarette smoking is the chief way tobacco is used, the bulk of what has been said has been about cigarettes. You probably already know a great deal about cigarette smoking. Test your knowledge by the following questions:

	True	False
1. Cigarettes don't hurt young people.	___	___
2. Filters make cigarettes safe.	___	___
3. Most doctors don't smoke.	___	___
4. The more cigarettes you smoke the bigger risk you take.	___	___
5. There is some question whether or not cigarettes are harmful.	___	___
6. Lung cancer is the only disease associated with smoking cigarettes.	___	___
7. Young people can quit smoking easier than adults who have smoked a long time.	___	___

Knowing the following facts about tobacco will help you answer these questions and make the right decision concerning smoking.

The Pressure Is Great

There is pressure on many young people to smoke. You probably feel some of that pressure. A person is more likely to smoke if his parents and friends smoke; there is a subtle push to join in. Cigarette advertising pictures smoking as a pleasant, even beautiful, practice and makes it very appealing.

Some young people feel that smoking shows they are no longer children. Many boys seem to believe that smoking makes them appear more masculine. Puffing on a cigarette may also satisfy the sucking instinct which is a carry-over from infancy. Smoking a cigarette is kin to sucking a pacifier.

Once a person begins to smoke he is likely to continue. Some people can smoke a few cigarettes and not get the tobacco habit. But most persons cannot limit themselves to a few cigarettes. The habit is quickly established and smoking becomes part of a daily routine. Research reveals that the person who begins to smoke a few cigarettes as a teen-ager is likely to become a habitual smoker. The best way to avoid getting hooked on cigarettes is never to smoke one.

Smoking Is Harmful

Some persons feel that smoking is a petty issue. But the United States government, the American Cancer Society, the American Heart Association, the American Medical Association, and others consider smoking a major health problem. Scientific studies show beyond any reasonable doubt that smoking cigarettes is harmful to health. Doctors know cigarette smoking is harmful; over 100,000 doctors quit smoking soon after the special studies linking smoking and poor health were published.

Smoking is closely linked to various diseases of the lungs and throat. The so-called "smokers' cough" is one evidence of the irritation to the respiratory system caused by tobacco. Emphysema, a disease in which the victim often chokes to death on his own body fluids, occurs mainly in smokers. Cancers of the mouth are more frequent in smokers than nonsmokers.

Such cancers are often treated by cutting away the mouth and part of the face, leaving an ugly gaping hole. Lung cancer is ten times as high among regular smokers as among those who never smoked. For those who smoke two packs a day the rate is twenty times as high.

Cigarettes are closely related to heart disease. Death rates from heart attacks in men are from 50 to 200 percent higher among smokers than nonsmokers. The degree depends on age and number of cigarettes smoked. Diseases of the circulatory system are much more frequent in smokers than nonsmokers. Sometimes circulation is cut down so much that toes, fingers, and limbs must be amputated.

Smokers suffer a higher rate of several other health problems than nonsmokers. Ulcer of the stomach and cirrhosis of the liver are two of the most prevalent. Smoking also seems to slow down the rate of healing from disease. Smokers are sick more often, suffer more restrictions due to ill health, and are confined to bed more than are nonsmokers.

The sicknesses related to smoking cut down on life expectancy. Smokers have a higher death rate than nonsmokers. Cigarette smokers tend to die younger than those who do not smoke. Sickness and death related to smoking vary according to three factors: when the smoking began, how many cigarettes a day are smoked, and whether the smoke is inhaled. A person who begins inhaling a pack or two of cigarettes a day when he is under twenty is the most likely to develop serious, painful disease and die early. The death rate, for example, of persons who begin smoking when fifteen years of age is twice as high as for those who never smoke.

The harm caused by smoking is very costly. Many work days are lost due to smoking-related illness. People who smoke miss more work time than those who do not. In a recent year over *470 million* work days were lost because of illness related to smoking. Premature deaths of workers also are expensive since persons must be trained to take their places.

Health costs must also be added to the smoking bill. According to the Public Health Service, smoking results in more than

1 million extra cases of chronic bronchitis or emphysema, 1.8 million extra cases of serious sinus infection, 1 million extra cases of peptic ulcer, and 300,000 extra heart attacks. The large increase in lung cancer seems related to cigarette smoking. Conditions in already overcrowded medical facilities are made worse by these extra illnesses due to smoking.

Smoking is damaging and costly in other ways. Cigarettes often stain teeth and fingers. The smoke from cigarettes fouls the air, and the odor clings to clothing and furniture. Fires started from the matches or cigarettes of smokers burn forests, houses, clothes, and buildings. In addition to the tens of thousands who die from smoking-related diseases, others are burned to death in these fires.

Anyone Can Stop

It may be difficult, but anyone who really wants to stop smoking can do so. The longer a person smokes the more difficult it is for him to stop. For example, a young person can quit the habit easier than an adult who has been smoking for years. But anyone can stop.

A dependence on tobacco develops in the smoker. Smoking for some people soothes nerves and relieves tension. It may make a person feel more poised. Smoking gives the smoker something to do with his hands. It is easy to see how a smoker develops a yearning for cigarettes. Strong determination and will power are demanded to break the habit.

It is worth whatever it costs to break the habit. A person reaps rich rewards for giving up smoking. His sense of taste and smell improves. Food tastes better. If he has been sneaky in his smoking he can stop being dishonest. He feels better and his teeth are brighter.

He saves money. The money spent on cigarettes could be used for more worthwhile things. A moderate to heavy smoker in an average lifetime will spend money on cigarettes equal to the cost of a large house, or dozens of trips to other countries, or the finest college education, or several luxury automobiles.

In athletics and studies his performance will likely improve.

Smoking drags an athlete's performance down. That is why the best coaches and stars are against cigarette smoking. The athlete who excels even though he smokes could do better if he did not. And since smoking reduces mental ability, it can detract from study.

The person who stops smoking improves his health. Even though he has been smoking for a long time, to stop is to improve his health. The body is very effective in getting rid of poisons. If given a chance, it can heal much of the damage done by tobacco. When a person quits smoking he increases the prospects of living a longer and healthier life. After about ten years the death rates of persons who stop smoking are almost the same as for those who never smoked.

Stopping smoking may improve relations with others. Smoking is frequently irritating to others. Many nonsmokers do not appreciate having their clothes, car, and house fouled with tobacco odor. Cigarette burns on carpets, furniture, and clothes are not only costly in money but also in good will.

Some people try means other than quitting to cut down the damage done by cigarettes. Many use filter cigarettes. Others reduce the number of cigarettes they smoke per day. Some smoke only part of the cigarette. None of these common practices eliminates the danger of smoking. Nicotine and other damaging substances in cigarettes still get into the body. The best way to prevent damage from cigarettes is never to smoke. The second best is to stop.

Think About It

What do you think is the right response to tobacco in the light of these facts? Review the questions at the first of this chapter and see if you answered them correctly. The answers can be found in this chapter. In addition to the true and false questions, here are some other questions to help you think through the issues of smoking:

Why do people smoke cigarettes? Are any of these reasons strong enough to justify smoking in the light of the facts about it?

How do you hurt yourself when you smoke?

Why do leading coaches not want athletes to smoke?

Do you think you can do your best for God if you smoke?

In what ways could you hurt others by smoking?

How does the Christian concept of stewardship relate to smoking?

What arguments can be given in defense of smoking? in opposition to smoking?

What distinctly Christian reasons can be given for not smoking?

When someone offers you a cigarette or urges you to smoke, remember: Anyone can say yes, but it takes backbone to say no. And the most dangerous time to start smoking is when you are young.

13. Gambling

More money is spent on gambling in the United States than on education, medical care, or religion. Billions of dollars are wagered each year. Gambling is not a petty issue. And it involves millions of young people.

As you know, many young people flip coins for drinks, play cards for small stakes, make bets on sports events, or play games of chance at carnivals. Some also get involved in hardcore gambling—betting on horses, buying lottery tickets, playing slot machines, going to gambling casinos.

Why People Gamble

Why do people gamble? The reasons vary from person to person. Some gamble because their friends urge them to. Rather than be left out or made fun of, they take part. When everyone else in a group agrees to flip for drinks or play cards for money it may be hard not to go along.

Others gamble because it is exciting and fun. They feel that betting on the outcome of a game makes it more interesting. Winning makes a person happy. Losing usually brings anger or depression. But win or lose, emotion runs high. It is easy to see why people who are bored frequently turn to gambling for excitement. Some come to depend on gambling for excitement. They become compulsive gamblers.

You may know someone who keeps gambling even though he almost always loses. Strange as it seems, some people gamble because they want to lose. They have a desire to be punished, to be hurt. Since very few ever win in gambling, it fills a need in their lives. Such people are suffering from emotional sickness and need special help.

Gambling attracts many because it offers a way to get rich quick with no work and little effort. Even when the stakes are not large, gambling promises something for nothing—or for very little. Give-aways, prizes, and so-called free offers in advertising have made "something for nothing" a widely accepted idea in America.

Arguments in Defense of Gambling

A number of arguments are used to defend gambling. Some people claim that gambling is merely a form of recreation. They suggest that many people pay money to see a movie, a play, or a football game; others pay to gamble. They don't play to win, necessarily, just to enjoy the thrill of gambling—so the argument goes. But is recreation to be judged only on the basis of fun? Aren't other factors also to be considered, such as the harm done to persons or to society? Isn't it important to ask, "Does the recreation build a better or a worse world?"

Others argue that gambling is not wrong because all of life is a risk. But aren't the risks in gambling different from the risks in ordinary life? There are risks in business, farming, or driving a car. But aren't these risks necessary? And doesn't the businessman, farmer, or driver rely on something more than chance—training, hard work, skill, for example? Also, doesn't he attempt to reduce the risk element to the minimum? On the other hand, the risk in gambling is not necessary for our well-being and the true gambler relies on nothing more than chance.

Some believe that the desire to gamble is part of human nature. They argue that since this is true, it is useless to prohibit gambling. But no one has proved that the gambling urge is part of human nature. Even if it is, do you think a person should be allowed to do whatever comes naturally? What kind of world do you think we would have if we followed this line of reasoning?

Some people defend gambling as a means of raising money for governments, churches, and other groups. In some places gambling is already used this way. But couldn't money raised by gambling be raised by means not harmful to persons? As the Los Angeles Chief of Police said, "A society that bases its financial structure on the weakness of its people doesn't deserve to survive."

Problems with Gambling

A study of the facts reveals many problems about gambling. Hopefully the following facts will help you in deciding what to do about gambling:

Gambling contributes to crime. The crime rate in America, already dangerously high, continues to increase. One reason for this increase seems to be widespread gambling. Gambling and crime usually go hand in hand. For example, Nevada, considered the gambling capital of the nation, has a per capita crime rate double the national average. The states with legalized gambling have crime rates twice as high as those states with no legalized gambling. When asked, "Is there a connection between gambling and crime?" an Assistant United States Attorney General replied, "Yes. It's a man on a meat hook we discovered in a San Francisco warehouse. It's a man in a car dynamited in Cleveland, Ohio. Maybe he deserved it, but his thirteen-year-old son didn't deserve to be blinded for life."

Gambling helps support the activities of America's underworld. Profits from gambling finance organized crime. A Senate committee studying gambling and organized crime stated that "the chief source of revenue for organized crime is illegal gambling." The committee also indicated that "the huge profits from illegal gambling were the primary source of funds to finance other activities of organized crime." There is evidence that organized crime also benefits from legal gambling activities.

Gambling corrupts government officials. Professional gamblers bribe policemen, public officials, athletes, and referees. Those who take such bribes often feel shame, and some have had their careers ruined. A lawyer who headed a special government study of organized crime declared, "Fully half of the syndicate's income from gambling is earmarked for protection money paid to police and politicians." Money bet just for fun can help corrupt and destroy decent government.

Gambling hurts the people involved. It stimulates a something-for-nothing craving which undermines character. Some steal to get money for gambling. Gambling develops bad character traits—recklessness, covetousness, and callousness. Those who can least afford to lose—the poor—are usually the most vulnerable to the lure of gambling. No one expects to become a compulsive gambler. But approximately one out of ten persons who gamble get to the point where they cannot control their desire to gamble. The so-called petty gambler is flirting with disaster.

Gambling harms innocent people. As one member of Gamblers Anonymous stated, "It is difficult to say whether the gambler or his wife is the more physically, mentally, and emotionally damaged by the ravages of a gambling binge." Child neglect and divorce are frequently related to gambling. Money needed for groceries and rent all too often goes for gambling. Innocent bystanders are sometimes hurt when violence breaks out over gambling.

Gambling is a drag on the economy. Many business and labor leaders oppose gambling because it works against the best interests of almost everyone. A labor spokesman has stated that most labor organizations oppose commercialized gambling because of its "drag on the economy, diverting purchasing power from job-producing industries." A manager of a large department store in Los Angeles reported that "receipts of bad checks doubled during racing season, that absenteeism increased, and that time payments fell off as much as 30 per cent." Experience shows that an increase in unpaid bills, embezzlement, bankruptcy, and absenteeism goes along with an increase in gambling.

Gambling is for suckers. The professional gambler really does not gamble. The odds are prearranged so that the professional wins and the others involved lose. In most legalized gambling operations the professional's profit is from 15 to 60 percent. In illegal operations it is usually much higher.

Gambling violates biblical principles. The Bible contains no specific command about gambling. But gambling is contrary to the spirit of the Scriptures. The Bible stresses the sovereignty of God in life (Matt. 10:29–30); gambling is based on chance and luck. The Bible is opposed to covetousness and materialism (Matt. 6:19–34); both are basic in the desire to gamble. The Bible condemns theft (Matt. 19:18); gambling is usually theft by mutual consent. The Bible stresses love for neighbor (Matt. 22:37–40); gambling seeks personal gain at the expense of one's neighbor. The Bible urges men to take part in honest, constructive work (Eph. 4:28; 2 Thess. 3:10–12); gambling stimulates a something-for-nothing outlook. The Bible calls for stewardship of life and possessions (Rom. 14:12; Col. 3:17); gambling undermines both the recognition and practice of stewardship.

How to Decide

In light of the facts, do you believe a Christian should gamble? Of course, there is a difference in flipping a coin to determine who will pay for the cokes and placing bets with a bookie on a horse race. But aren't petty gambling and hardcore gambling basically alike in nature? And isn't there a chance that small-time gambling will lead to more destructive practices?

Answering the following questions may help you come to a decision on what to do about gambling:

Will gambling help or harm me as a person?

Is gambling more likely to help or hurt other people?

What kind of a country would we have if everyone gambled?

Will gambling help me to become a better Christian?

Will gambling—even petty gambling—help or hinder my Christian witness to others?

Can I best show love for God, neighbor, and self by gambling or refusing to gamble?

If you decide not to gamble, you will face these additional questions:

How can I stay out of situations where the pressure to gamble will be great?

How can I refuse to gamble when urged to do so without sounding holier-than-thou?

How can I work to keep others from being hurt by gambling?

14. Dishonesty

"Tell it like it is." "Shoot straight with me." "What I like about him is that he's so honest." "Don't be a phoney." "He's nothing but a hypocrite."

Such statements by young people seem to reveal that they put great stock in honesty. You probably do. But don't you also know a number of young people who are dishonest? Of course, the delinquents and so-called bad kids are often dishonest. But we are talking also about those who are considered good guys. Let's take a look at some of the more common forms of dishonesty.

Cheating

Have you ever copied someone else's answer on a test? Maybe you just needed a hint to help you get started and looked. Or perhaps you did not know the answer at all but did not want to fail. Have you ever had someone ask to copy your test answers or your homework? What did you do? If yours is a typical school, cheating is a live issue. How many in your class do you think have at some time cheated? How many cheat fairly regularly? How many see little wrong with it?

Students give many explanations for cheating: "Teachers allow it. If some cheat, you have to cheat too in order not to be at a disadvantage." "Parents demand good grades and cheating is a common way to make them." "Almost everyone does it." "If you don't allow others to copy, they call you self-righteous or holier-than-thou." How do you feel these arguments stand up in light of the Christian principles set forth in Part I?

Cheating takes many forms: copying someone else's test paper or assignment, stealing copies of exams or keys to textbooks and workbooks, finding out what questions are on a test from someone who has taken it before. Whatever form it takes when you cheat, don't you profess to know something you don't really know? Don't you pretend to have done something you did not do? When you cheat, don't you lie, steal, and act like a hypocrite? Aren't all forms of cheating dishonest?

Cheating harms the cheater. He doesn't learn what he should. Sooner or later his lack of knowledge will catch up with him. Cheating usually causes anxiety; there is always the danger of being caught. If you are caught you might fail the course or have a note attached to your permanent school record about your cheating. Such a record may stand in the way of future opportunities and even prevent you from entering a particular college or vocation.

Cheating can damage others. Someone may follow your example and be hurt by cheating. Or you may harm someone because you didn't learn what you needed to know since you cheated. Would you like to be cared for by a doctor who cheated his way through medical school? Would you like to ride in a plane worked on by an engineer who cheated in his engineering courses? What kind of a world would we have if everyone were a cheater?

Most important, perhaps, will cheating hurt or help your spiritual life and the cause of Christ? Do you believe a cheat can be as effective a witness for Christ as an honest student can be? Apply the three questions discussed in chapter 5 to cheating: "Will cheating harm me? Others? The cause of Christ?" What do you believe is right: to cheat or not to cheat?

Lying

When you were a little child you probably sometimes found it hard to distinguish between fiction and fact. You told make-believe stories as if they were really true. As you grew up, you learned to distinguish between fact and fiction. But some young people are still like little children in that they tell false stories as if they were true.

People tell lies in many different ways and for a variety of reasons. Some lie in order to stay out of trouble. They do something wrong and then lie to cover up. One lie leads to another and soon the person is hopelessly tangled in the web of his own untruth. Others lie by exaggeration, usually to get attention. They tell a story that is basically true but add so much color that it becomes false. "Little lies" are used to avoid hurting someone's feelings. For example, a girl asks a boy how he likes her new dress, and he says, "Just fine!" when he really thinks it looks terrible on her.

Some forms of lying are very subtle. A person can lie by a nod of his head or a look in his eye. For example, someone can ask if you have done a particular thing and by nodding your head you can indicate that you have when you have not. Or by creating a look of attention in your eye you can make a person feel that you are concentrating on what he is saying when in reality you are not.

Some lies are more destructive than others. People sometimes spread lies about others in order to hurt them. But all lies are potentially harmful. If a person gets in the habit of lying, no one believes what he says or takes him seriously. He may have something important to share which would save others from being hurt, but he is not believed. Lying destroys trust which persons should have for one another. Lying, therefore, can hurt you and others.

Read chapter 7 again and consider lying from the standpoint of the three sources of light. What does your conscience tell you about telling a lie? How do people you admire feel about lying? What does the Bible say about the false witness and the liar? Do you feel that the practice of lying is in harmony with God's will? Do you want people to lie to you?

Stealing

When we started out to write this book we did not plan a section on stealing. But a number of young people urged us to include it. They insisted that stealing is widespread among young people. Do you agree?

The poor sometimes steal for food and clothes. But why do those who are not poor steal? Many car thieves and shoplifters come from homes where the young people have all the things that they need. Some who steal hubcaps, road signs, and school property don't need the items they take. Why do they steal? For the thrill? To brag about it to others? Because they think it is smart? To get money for drugs?

People steal for different reasons. But the result and effect is the same whatever the reason. Stealing costs. It costs other people. Parents are hurt when a son or daughter is a thief. The person from whom something is stolen must pay to replace it. Sometimes the cost is passed on to other people. Store owners have to charge higher prices because of shoplifting. Taxes are higher because people steal state property such as road signs and school materials.

Stealing costs the thief. Often he is arrested and then fined or jailed. Even if he is not caught, he suffers from fear of being caught. Many thieves are troubled by a guilty conscience. Some are blackmailed by people who know that they have stolen.

Stealing hurts society. Can you imagine how terrible it would be to live in a society of thieves? Everything would have to be guarded closely all the time. Wouldn't it be better to live in a society where you could leave things out in the open without fear of someone taking them?

Review chapter 5 and apply the three tests to the issue of stealing: Would you be ashamed to be seen stealing by your parents, teachers, or pastor? Would you be willing for everyone to steal? Could you sincerely ask God to bless you as you steal?

In light of these tests what do you believe about shoplifting? Picking up property you find which someone has left out in the open? Taking money from your parents without asking? Removing road signs and other public property—just for kicks? Carrying off towels from a motel as a souvenir? Keeping the extra money when someone gives you the wrong change?

Making Up Your Mind

Other types of dishonesty and lawbreaking by youth may be common in your community, such as violating traffic laws, purchasing alcohol under age, possessing marijuana, and defacing property. The principles set forth in Part I can be applied to these issues, too.

A growing number of people seem to feel that being honest about being dishonest excuses the act. What do you think?

"Honesty is the best policy" is an old saying. Do you believe it is true? Many people do. Honesty does not mean being crude, rude, blunt, or hurtful, as some seem to think. Honesty does not require that you tell a person all that you think about him or share all that you know about a situation. Such talk might do more harm than good. But honesty does require a basic pattern of life in which you don't misrepresent yourself, take what is not yours, deliberately state what is untrue, or break the law for personal gain. Are you basically an honest person?

15. Sex

Fire when properly used warms cold rooms, cooks food, and welds metal. Wrongly used it can burn and destroy. Sex in many ways is like fire. It must be respected and used correctly or it will damage and destroy. Sex is one of the major issues many of you face in regard to what is right or wrong. A basic drive in the human race, sex is a gift from God and essentially good. But like any other drive or gift, it can be misused.

Thoughts and Daydreams

It is only natural that thoughts about sex pop into your mind. A maturing boy who didn't admire a pretty girl or a maturing girl who wasn't impressed by a handsome boy would be less than normal. And often a person will find himself daydreaming about being with someone to whom he is attracted. Such daydreaming in itself is perfectly healthy.

When thoughts and daydreams begin to center almost exclusively on sexual themes, however, you need to put your mind to work on other things. You cannot control what thoughts enter your mind, but you can control what you allow to linger. Some youth spend hours in daydreams about sexual exploits. When such images come in a wet dream at night, there is nothing for a boy to be ashamed of; he has no control over this. But young men and women can control daydreams.

How you think about sex is important. Since sex is a good gift from God, it should be treated with respect in thought as well as action. Have you noticed how, in general, outer action is often the result of inner thoughts and attitudes? This means that a person should not dwell in his mind on any activity which he would be ashamed to carry out in the open.

Conversation and Jokes

For some people sex plays a big role in their conversation. Regardless of what subject is being discussed, they manage to bring in sex. Some talk about sex is helpful—when it is factual and wholesome. Sharing Christian convictions about sex, for example, can strengthen those convictions. Talk about sex, even on a high plane, is often sexually stimulating, however; if a boy and girl are talking they should be very careful.

Unfortunately, much talk about sex is cheap and degrading. You have probably heard people brag about sexual conquests —real and imagined—share misunderstanding about sex, tell jokes which picture sex as dirty or crude, or treat sex lightly. Such talk drags a holy gift of God into the gutter. Discussions about sex should always be helpful. This calls for factual statements which picture sex as a gift from God to be used responsibly for the welfare of all persons.

Books, Movies, Television

Some books, movies, and television shows which deal with sex are helpful. They are produced for the specific purpose of leading people to deal with sex in a healthy, Christian way. But many books, movies, and television shows which deal with sex do it to exploit your sexual drive in order to make money. They have no helpful word to say. And in most cases the kind of life they picture leads to grief and unhappiness.

Books and movies with vivid sex scenes can create problems for you. You may find that such scenes stick in your mind and keep coming into your thoughts again and again. Descriptions of what the sex act is like may give you a false impression which can cause difficulty later in sexual adjustment in marriage. Most important, perhaps, is that the attitude toward sex in these books and movies is far below Christian standards. You may accept these standards if you frequently expose yourself to them.

Dress

Clothing, in general, in addition to making us more comfortable is intended to curtail sexual desire. The sex drive is so powerful and so quickly triggered, especially in men, that most people would find it very difficult to carry on normal daily routines among unclothed people. Thus "sexy" dress defeats one of the purposes for clothes; it is distracting.

Dress which makes a person pleasantly attractive, on the other hand, is helpful, not harmful. Custom and culture have much to do with what is good taste in dress and what is not. The Bible also indicates that a Christian should dress modestly in a way not to call attention to himself.

Dating

Dating is for fun, but it is also to help young men and women learn to get along with and understand each other. It is supposed to be part of preparation for marriage. A person should learn through dating how to make plans, carry on a conversation, and work out disagreements. Sex is basic to dating, of course. Dating does not begin until the sex drive develops. But dating must involve more than sex if it is to prepare you for marriage and adulthood.

The first dates often are in a group. Later, single dating develops. The age at which you begin to date is something you need to work out with your parents. But remember that many people make the mistake of starting too young.

A young person should date many different people. This will help him learn how to get along with others and discover the type person with whom he would be most compatible in marriage. Going steady robs a person of the opportunity to date many different people. It also gets him more deeply entangled emotionally than most youth can handle well.

Petting

For some couples, dating centers almost exclusively on the physical. Regardless of what they start out to do, each date ends the same way. Petting is the main event. For some it involves only embracing and kissing. For others, just about every physical contact short of sexual intercourse is involved. The following facts about petting may be helpful as you decide what to do about it:

Petting is habit forming. A couple can quickly get into a pattern of spending most of their time petting. The pattern is difficult to break. It robs the couple of much that dating can contribute to their lives.

Petting is frequently dishonest. It often expresses a degree of affection which the persons do not really have for one another. Sometimes one person may be expressing real affection, while the other is using him or her only for selfish sexual enjoyment.

Petting reduces sex to the physical. It keeps a couple from learning how to relate to one another as total persons. It makes for shallow relations. People who spend most of their time petting don't really learn much about one another. Marriages built almost exclusively on the physical are on a shaky foundation.

Petting can create guilt. A person who believes his body is a temple of the Holy Spirit will not be happy allowing it to be used for selfish pleasure.

Heavy petting can cause emotional disorder. It leaves no good way out. Petting in God's plan for human sexuality is designed to prepare a male and female for sexual intercourse. When a couple pet, they trigger physical and emotional reactions which gear the body for going all the way. To stop short is like throwing a car into reverse while it is moving forward —it's damaging. On the other hand, to go all the way will be even more harmful. The only way not to hurt one another is not to get involved in heavy petting.

Properly controlled expressions of genuine affection which are not designed to lead to deeper sexual activity or to intercourse can be all right for a Christian. But anything else seems out of bounds sexually for a child of God who practices personal responsibility.

Sexual Intercourse

As you know, many unmarried young people have sexual intercourse. Some get involved in heavy petting, fail to put on the brakes, and go all the way even when they didn't plan to. Others have accepted the idea that there is nothing wrong with premarital sexual intercourse if two people really care for each other, want to have sex, and no one else gets hurt. A few even claim that premarital relations make for a stronger marriage later. What are the facts? Here are some to consider.

Going all the way involves real risk of pregnancy. Some people claim that birth control pills and other contraceptives have eliminated this risk. Such is not the case. Births out of wedlock, girls pregnant at their weddings, and abortions number in the millions each year—each one representing an unwanted pregnancy. One sure way to avoid out-of-wedlock conception is not to go all the way.

Disease can also result from sexual intercourse. Venereal disease is at epidemic rates in many sections of the United States. Venereal disease affects not only those who have the disease but others as well. For example, a child can be born blind or retarded to a person who has syphilis. What do you think about someone who would do a thing like that to an innocent child? The best way to avoid venereal disease is to steer clear of premarital sexual intercourse.

Sexual relations prior to marriage can cause emotional problems. Guilt is often created. This guilt may not surface until years later. Sometimes it disrupts a marriage and thereby hurts a number of people. In other cases the emotional harm shows up right away. Guilt, fear of pregnancy and disease, and the trauma of breaking up with someone who has been a sex partner can lead to personality changes, poor grades, distraction, and severe emotional disorder.

Sex affects the total personality. At its best it involves love and marriage. To claim, as some do, that sexual intercourse is no more significant than eating or drinking reveals vast misunderstanding of the nature and effect of sexual intercourse.

Human sex without love, trust, and commitment falls far short of what God intends for man and hurts the persons involved. Casual sex reduces man to the level of animals.

Going all the way before marriage violates clear biblical teaching (see 1 Cor. 6:15–20; Rev. 22:15). God wants us to have the joy that comes from following his will about sex. His restrictions are not to keep us from being happy but to help us find real happiness in all of life.

Other Issues

Other matters related to sex concern many young people. You may have wondered, for example, about masturbation. This practice is common among young people. It does not cause any physical harm unless practiced very frequently. But it does often cause feelings of shame and guilt. If this is a problem for you, talk it over with a mature Christian.

Homosexuality is another problem related to sex which causes many young people great concern. You may know some people who are homosexuals. You may even have been urged by some to enter into some homosexual practice with them. The Bible indicates that this kind of sex is contrary to God's will (Rom. 1:26–27). Don't fall for the arguments favoring homosexuality or get involved, as some do, for the thrill of a different kind of experience. If you find that you have a stronger sexual attraction to someone of your own sex than to a person of the opposite sex, talk immediately with a Christian leader and seek professional help.

Steps to Decision

How you handle the basically good, God-given sexuality which is yours will to a large degree determine the happiness of your life. In regard to various sexual activities apply the following questions:

Will this practice harm me physically, emotionally, mentally, or spiritually? Will it harm others? Will it harm the cause of Christ? (See chapter 5.)

Would I be willing for my parents and pastor to know I'm

doing this? Would I be willing for everybody to do this? Could I freely pray and ask God to bless me as I practice this? (See chapter 6.)

What does my conscience tell me about this? What is the advice of mature Christians who have my best interest at heart? What does the Bible say about this issue? What do I sincerely believe God wants me to do? (See chapter 7.)

Keep in mind that your decisions about these issues may differ greatly from those of non-Christians. You have a different set of values from them. You may seem to miss out on a lot of fun and you may be kidded because of your convictions. But take a look at the difference in the lives of people in happy, Christian homes and those who have played loose with sex. Isn't it clear that God's ways are always best for us?

16. Parents

Putting parents in a lineup with narcotics, alcohol, and gambling may surprise you. We don't really consider parents to be moral problems. But relations with parents call for some serious decision making. Your entire future may rest on how well you handle these decisions. Most young people realize this. In surveys many youth indicate that their relations to parents is one of the things that bother them most. There is a right way and a wrong way to relate to parents.

In some families parent-youth relations are marred by shouting, pouting, teasing, nagging, and door slamming. In others, although things are not always perfect, everyone generally enjoys family life. Trust, understanding, and good times are part of the daily scene. What makes the difference? Normally, it is that members of the family work at making family life happy.

Happy homes don't just happen. It takes planning, thought, talking together, and hard work. Parents can't do the job all alone. They need the help of their children. That is where you come in. (Of course, you can't make a happy home alone either. You need the cooperation of parents, brothers, and sisters.) Here are some ways many young people have found to improve the relation with their parents.

Understand Yourself

First, understand yourself. You are undergoing some rapid changes which affect your entire life. Some of these changes are physical. Rapid growth is tiring and sometimes painful. You may feel tired and irritable part or much of the time.

There is frequently some anxiety over physical change, too. Girls are anxious about being pretty and boys about being strong and reasonably good looking. Sometimes the preoccupation of young people with grooming gets on the nerves of parents and younger brothers and sisters.

Closely related to physical changes are emotional ones. Strong new feelings emerge. Often you have little experience to guide you in these emotions. This may make you unsure so that you overreact. Anger, temper flareups, and moodiness are frequently the result. Many young people can correctly be labeled "tween-agers"; they are between being children and being adults. One moment they act like responsible adults and the next like unpredictable children.

Emotional difficulties are sometimes intensified by outside pressures. Increasing demands are made on you as you grow older. You may long for the carefree days of a little kid. School becomes more difficult and important as college and future job opportunities depend on grades. Social life is fun but it often throws you in the middle of new and difficult experiences. At home you are expected to assume more and more responsibility. All of this is part of growing up. But sometimes you may feel like you are living in a pressure cooker.

Even your spiritual life may be upsetting. Questioning and doubt are often part of the religious life of a young person. Comforting, cherished beliefs may no longer seem believable. At the same time religious impressions are more meaningful. Deep doubt and great faith may come in waves leaving a young person disturbed.

In order to develop into a mature person you need love, discipline, supervision, security, and a sense of belonging. Without these you are headed for trouble. Antisocial, emotionally disturbed people almost always lack these elements in their homes. Yet many young people tend to reject these.

All of this means you may have a tendency to be moody, explosive, critical, self-centered, and/or questioning—traits which don't make a person easy to live with. You have to work extra hard to be the kind of person who makes family life fun.

Understand Your Parents

It is also helpful to understand your parents if you want a good relation with them. Remember, parents are people. Even the best are not perfect! Like all people, they have their strong and weak points, their good and bad days, their hopes and fears. They do not know all the answers. But most of them try to be good parents.

Many fathers are under extra stress and severe pressures. Knowing about this will help you to understand why a dad sometimes acts the way he does. A job, for example, may be a point of tension for a father. Many men old enough to be the parent of a person your age are at a critical time in their jobs. In some cases young men with new ideas and boundless energy threaten the job security of older men.

Fathers are also often bothered by money problems. As children grow older they become more expensive. Frequently a father's income does not go up as fast as expenses. When his family wants something that he cannot afford, it may make him feel that he is a failure. Frustrated and depressed, he may lash out at others, even those he loves.

Mothers also need understanding. If a mother works in a job outside the home, she may face similar pressures and frustrations to that of a man. If she is strictly a homemaker, she may feel unappreciated and suffer from the "I'm just a housewife" blues.

Many mothers of young people are going through a change in life called menopause. This is the time when the monthly cycle of ovulation and menstruation ceases. The woman is no longer able to become pregnant and give birth. Her body chemistry, long adjusted for motherhood, goes through disrupting changes. Often this has both a physical and an emotional impact on her. She may become more irritable and tense than usual. In some families while the mother is losing her ability to bear children, her daughter is developing the potential for motherhood. Both are undergoing radical, disrupting changes. This can create an explosive situation.

Both parents may be dealing with the realization that they are no longer young. They are having to adjust to the fact that all of their dreams and hopes are not going to be realized. They may feel hemmed in by responsibilities. For youth, everything seems possible; they can dream of the things they will do in the future. But middle-aged adults know that much of what they as young people had dreamed of doing they will never do. In some ways, usually subconscious, parents may envy or be jealous of their own children even though they love them dearly.

Mothers and fathers suffer the normal fears and anxieties of life. In addition, they have a special concern for you. As you grow older, their anxiety often mounts. It is not necessarily that they don't trust you. It is due at least in part to their realization that your potenial for good and evil has vastly increased since you were a little child. When you were younger about all you could do damagewise was fall out of a tree, wreck your bike, or get a bloody nose in a fight. Now you can kill someone with a car, be involved in a crime, get hooked on drugs, be part of giving birth to a child, or join a revolution.

Most parents are also concerned about doing what is best for you. But they are not always sure what is best. And you probably don't always agree with their point of view. They want you to do well in school, but they don't want to push you beyond your ability. They would like for you to have many friends, but they don't want you to forsake principle for popularity. Being the parent of a young person is not easy.

Understand Parent-Youth Relations

During the next few years your parents will be working to move you to independence. Getting you on your own is not a simple matter. And the process can be stormy. They know that it is only normal for you to grow up and leave home yet they also would like to keep you with them. So they may at one time be possessive and at another push you hard toward independence.

You, too, probably have mixed feelings about growing up. Mostly, you are eager to be on your own. But sometimes the comfort and security of home are appealing. If your parents are feeling possessive at the time you are wanting independence, relations are likely to be difficult.

Most parents do not know exactly how fast to let their children move toward independence. Bird parents seem to have a knack for knowing when bird children are ready to leave the nest. When this time comes, the bird parents push the little birds out and they flap, flap away. But human parents don't have this kind of natural insight. They must work by trial and error.

The ideal approach is for a parent to give a little freedom and observe how the young person responds. If he does well, they should give him more rope and grant a bit more freedom. If he misuses the freedom, they must draw in the rope. This can be a frustrating and sometimes painful experience for everybody involved. But this kind of trial and error approach leads to enlarged experience and maturity. If you understand what is going on, you may be able to relate better to your parents than if you are unaware of the process.

You Can Make a Difference

In some families disputes develop between parents and youth. When disagreements arise, what should young people do? There is no simple, one-shot solution. What you should do depends on many things—the issue, your age, the personality of you and your parents, and your general relation with your parents. Here are some suggestions which many young people have found helpful in working out disputes. They may also be useful in keeping things running smoothly on a day-to-day basis.

Try to understand why your parents feel and act the way they do.

Respect your parents even when you disagree with them.

Recall the good times you have had together and note your parents' good qualities.

Keep the lines of communication open. Talk things over. Don't explode; instead, be patient.

Talk to counselors, teachers, and Christian friends about serious difficulties. Don't seek sympathy but help in coming to a positive solution.

Take an objective look at yourself to see in what ways you are contributing to family problems.

Be forgiving when your parents are at fault. Don't hold a grudge.

Pray about the problem. Pray for your parents. Ask God to help you control your emotions and guide your thinking.

Love your parents in word and deed. Read 1 Corinthians 13 often and try to measure up to the standard of love set forth there.

NOTE: Part of the material in this chapter is from *No Greater Challenge* by William M. Pinson, Jr., (Nashville: Convention Press, 1969), pp. 67–70. Used by permission.

17. Recreation

"What are you doing tonight?" "What have you got planned for this weekend?" When you ask these questions you probably don't have work in mind. You are talking about having fun, playing, breaking out of the daily routine. All work or all play makes for a dull life. A balance is much better. But it is not always easy to know what the right recreation is.

Purpose and Possibilities

Some people think that the purpose of recreation is to refresh you for more effective work. It should. But that is not the main reason people should play. People have been created by God with the need to relax, have fun, and play. It is just as important for your well-being to know how to play well as it is to work effectively.

What do you feel should be involved in good recreation? Here are some characteristics which some feel to be important: enjoyable; creative in that it calls for self-expression; constructive, not causing harm to anyone involved; different from your school or job activity; releasing in that you are able to lose yourself in it, be so caught up in it that you forget your problems. Most find that it is also wise to participate rather than just be a spectator. In short, it should contribute to your all-around good physical and mental health.

You probably give a lot of thought to what vocation you should enter. It is important also to consider carefully your recreation. There are many kinds of recreation available. Some are better than others and a few may be harmful or dangerous. Don't you feel that it would be better for you to decide what recreation is right for you rather than just to go along with the crowd?

You may find this chapter more meaningful if you will list all types of recreation available to you—good and bad. What is included in such a list will vary according to where you live, but these are some of the items you might include: sports, games, concerts, books, television, movies, parties, picnics, riding around in cars, banquets, plays, hiking, camp outs, dancing, clubs, carnivals and fairs, hobbies, art, crafts, and music. Some activities on your list may allow you to be either a spectator or a participant. For example, you can either help to stage a play or watch it. Other types of activity can be subdivided into many specifics. Sports, for example, can include a multitude of different possibilities—football, baseball, archery, swimming, water and snow skiing, basketball, hockey, hunting, ice skating, soccer, fishing, roller skating, tennis, golf, rowing, boxing, wrestling, track, cycling, auto racing, and others. There are also many different games and hobbies. Make your list as long as you can.

In the face of so many possibilities, how can a Christian know what is best for him to do? The following items may be helpful to you: the time, place, participants, and effect. Let's look at each of these.

Time

When an activity takes place is important in considering whether it is right or wrong. Wouldn't you agree that recreation should not conflict with basic responsibilities such as school, worship, and work? In other words, regardless of how wholesome an activity might be in itself, if it causes you to fail to live up to a responsibility, wouldn't it be questionable? Going on a picnic is in itself good recreation. But if you cut school to do it, couldn't this make it wrong? A ball game may be great fun. But if you miss Sunday Bible study and worship in order to go, wouldn't you fall short of your Christian commitment?

The amount of time spent in an activity will also have a bearing on whether it is right or wrong. If a person spends more hours in recreation or play than in study and work, wouldn't he likely be in error? You probably know some people who spend so much time at games or in sports that their school work suffers or they fail to take care of their responsibilities at home. Others are so caught up in certain activities that they don't get enough rest and damage their health. Riding around in a car talking with friends may not be a bad way to spend some free time. But if you stay out late night after night doing this, couldn't it become a harmful practice?

The impact on others is another factor to consider in relation to the time of an activity. A party with loud games might be all right in the afternoon, but what about late at night when people within earshot are trying to sleep? You may not think that going to a football game on Sunday will seriously damage your spiritual life, but what about a person who is looking your way for an example of a dedicated Christian? He might decide that you don't really believe your church is important after all. You may feel that going to a Sunday afternoon Walt Disney movie between church activities does you no harm, but what about the people who must work at the theater? Your support of Sunday movies may keep them from being able to participate in church services. Remember, one of the basic questions in Christian decision making is, "Will this practice harm others in any way?"

Place

The location of an activity is also an important factor in evaluating recreation. Some types of recreation are in themselves clean fun, but can become questionable in certain locations. Roller skating, for example, is good recreation. Unfortunately, a number of roller rinks are rough places where gangs, drinking, and drugs are present. Do you feel that skating in such a place would be wise? Other forms of recreation that may be questionable in themselves, such as dancing, are often made even more so by the location in which they are carried on. Even at well-chaperoned dances drinking is frequently a problem. At night clubs all sorts of difficulties exist for a Christian.

The location affects the rightness of recreation in another way. Certain activities are considered all right in some areas and wrong in others. Cards and bingo are acceptable games in many churches but considered sinful by others. Remember, a Christian should avoid doing something which is offensive or which might cause a weaker person to stumble. Something which is right may become wrong under certain circumstances. If you are in an area or among people where a specific activity is looked upon as wrong, don't you believe as a Christian you should avoid it? The sacrifice involved is a small price to pay for not offending sincere well-meaning persons.

Participants

Sometimes a decision on what to do about an activity may be based, at least in part, on who is participating. Riding around in a car is in itself harmless. But won't the persons who are driving and riding with you in the car determine to a large degree whether the activity is likely to be harmful? If the driver is drinking or on drugs or known to be reckless, don't you feel that it would be unwise to go along? If the others in the car are the kind of people who often are in trouble, then wouldn't it seem smart to excuse yourself?

For a young person, going on a date is a valid way to spend leisure time. But the rightness or wrongness of a particular date will depend largely on who is going. If a girl agrees to go with a boy she knows to be a wild driver, a fast operator in regard to sex, and/or a pot smoker, isn't she asking for trouble? Similarly, if a couple agree to go on a double date with another couple known for parking late on lonely roads, aren't they taking a big risk?

Your reputation and Christian witness may be hurt in recreation if you are part of a rough crowd. You may find it difficult to make friends with the "good guys" if you constantly run with "bad guys." Even the police and teachers may begin to watch you with suspicion. And before you are aware of it, some of the traits of your companions may rub off on you. You don't want to snub the people with shady reputations, of course. You may be able to help them. But can't you steer clear of participating regularly in recreational activity with them, particularly in a group?

Effect

The general effect of the activity is another thing to consider in deciding whether or not it is right to take part. Some activities have a built-in risk or harm. You probably recognize this is true, for example, in drinking alcohol, smoking pot, or gambling.

In other activities whether there is danger to you depends on how the recreation is carried on. Parties can be good clean fun. But when a party involves heavy drinking, loose sex, and an all night timetable, wouldn't you agree that it is bad news for a Christian? Playing football can be excellent recreation. But if it takes up too much time or is played dirty, doesn't it cease to be right for the child of God?

The effect of an activity on you may depend also on its content. Books, movies, plays, and television shows can be good or bad depending on their content. Many highlight violence, crude sex, and dishonesty. Some stir up prejudice or hatred. A steady diet of such material can warp a Christian's outlook. Don't you believe that good recreation should strengthen character and contribute to a better life? Isn't anything short of that undesirable?

The effect on other persons should be considered, too. Some activities threaten the welfare of others, even though they may be fun for you. High-speed driving on city streets or open highways falls into this category. It is possible for an activity to cause problems for others although you are not affected. Dancing, for example, to a girl is often merely a pleasant, relaxing activity with little or no sexual stimulation. However, some forms of dancing may overstimulate the sex drive of most boys and lead them into serious temptation. Going to certain movies may not harm you, but by your attendance you support an activity which may hurt someone else. Some clubs, fraternities, and sororities are so exclusive that they deeply hurt those who are not invited to join. Although the activities of such groups may not be immoral, their rude exclusiveness is.

Being Objective

Many of your most important decisions about right and wrong center in recreation. We suggest that you go over the list of possible activities which you made and carefully consider each one in light of this discussion and the principles set forth in Part I.

For each activity ask, "Will this be harmful to me? To others? To the cause of Christ?" Apply the three tests of chapter 6 to each: Secrecy—"Would I be ashamed to be seen doing this?" Universality—"Would I be willing for everyone to do this?" Prayer—"Can I ask God to bless me as I do this?" Seek the three sources of light set forth in chapter 7 for each: from without, within, and above.

Mark out those activities you believe to be outside God's will for your life and put a question mark by those you are not sure about. Out of those left unmarked pick a few to major on in your recreational activities as a Christian. Don't you really believe that your life will be better and you will have more fun in the long run by following Christian principles in your leisure time? And aren't there enough activities available to you so that you don't need to be part of those which are questionable?

18. Popularity

"She is the most popular girl in school" or "He is the most popular boy in the class" are common expressions. What do these expressions mean at your school or in your crowd? How is popularity measured? Is the most popular individual the one who is a member of the largest number of clubs and most frequently elected to offices, or is one's popularity measured in more general terms? Is the popular person in your school or community one who is generally well liked by others?

Popularity or Respect?

If popularity is measured in the latter way, it approaches rather closely to respect. How close it comes to genuine respect depends upon the basis for the so-called popularity. The popular individual may simply be a person who is friendly with everyone and hence everyone is friendly with him. This is a fine quality, but abiding respect is based on something deeper. It grows out of a conviction that the individual is genuine and dependable and that he has qualities of inner worth and dignity.

There is, to a degree, a sense of reverence mixed with this type of respect. There is a feeling that the individual possesses real character. Such respect derives primarily from what the individual is rather than what he does or how he looks. It is the respected individual who is the one sought when a real friend is needed.

The Christian can properly desire to be respected by others, even by those who may not agree with all he does or refuses to do. He should seek to win the respect of people by the consistent, effective life he lives for Christ. It should be his desire that when they need a real friend, they will turn to him for help.

We should remember, however, that our opportunities to help and to influence others will be limited if we are not friendly with all kinds of people. The Christian cannot live effectively for Christ if he separates himself from others, living his life in isolation. This is particularly true if this isolation involves a feeling of self-righteousness, a holier-than-thou attitude. There is a need for more Christian young people who will be uncompromisingly Christian, but at the same time they will be friendly with all kinds of young people—Christian, non-Christian, good, bad, and indifferent.

Popular or Unpopular?

"I do not care what anybody thinks." You have probably heard someone make such a statement. Do they really mean it? What has led them to say such a thing?

If we are normal, we do care what others think. One of our deepest desires is to be approved, particularly by those we love and respect. There may be a certain stage in our development when, on the surface, we do not seem to care what adults think about what we do. Down deep, however, we do care. There is at least one group whose approval we desire very much—our own age group or our gang. Sometimes we care so much about the latter that we practically become a slave to the group or gang, while at the same time we proclaim our freedom from all external control.

One who says he does not care what others think about him frequently has an inner conflict. He may want to do a certain thing that he knows will be disapproved by parents or friends. To justify his conduct he argues with himself, "I do not care what they think." Or, he may have a deep desire for popularity which he has failed to achieve. He rationalizes his failure by saying, "I don't care."

The latter young person may develop a martyr complex. He may seek to explain his lack of popularity by saying that one cannot be a consistent Christian and be popular. It must be admitted that there are some situations where this literally would be true. However, it is not the case in many groups, communities, and schools. There are some places where uncompromisingly Christian young people can be and are the most popular.

If we are not popular and not respected by most of our associates, should we not look within ourselves? If we look closely enough, we may discover that our lack of popularity has resulted from faults within our own personalities. It may be that we are proud and self-centered. We may be too determined to have our own way. We may be obsessed with a reformer complex. Or, we may have a spirit of self-righteousness. Whether popular or not, you can improve your personality so that you can be a more effective channel for service.

With or Without Compromise?

Popularity as such does not involve the problem of right or wrong. It is not necessarily right or wrong for you or any other young person to be popular. Many Christian young people have been very popular. Right and wrong may enter into the picture, however, in regard to the methods a person uses in an attempt to gain popularity, the place he gives to popularity in his life, or what he does with whatever popularity he may have.

Whether popularity is gained by means of or without compromise is one important factor in determining the rightness or wrongness of one's popularity. There are some schools, some communities, and certainly some groups where one can be popular without compromising basic principles or personal convictions. There are other places or groups where popularity would call for compromise by a Christian.

Any popularity that is gained through compromise of moral principles and spiritual ideals is purchased at too high a price. Such popularity ultimately is self-defeating. One cannot surrender his moral integrity without damaging, sooner or later, his total personality. For the Christian such compromise will result in inner condemnation by his own better self.

It should be remembered, however, that we are discussing the compromise of basic moral principles. If we are to get along with other people, we must not be contentious concerning unimportant or nonessential matters. Some Christians become offensive to their friends as well as to their enemies because they fail to see the difference between the essential and the nonessential. They are equally dogged in holding on to the less important and the more important. This is one way to lose friends and to fail to influence people.

It is possible for us to be uncompromising Christians and yet be agreeable, even with those with whom we may sharply differ. Most of us lose friends not so much because of what we stand for as the spirit and method with which we defend our position. The spirit of self-righteousness seems to be a rather distinctive temptation of Christians.

With Whom?

The rightness or wrongness of popularity may be determined to some degree by the ones with whom we are popular or desire to be popular. Usually, if one is popular with one group, he will be unpopular, to some extent, with other groups.

For example, rather serious questions should be raised concerning a Christian young person if he had become generally popular in his school but, at the same time, lost the respect of the best Christian young people. It would appear that he had paid a price for his popularity, a price that no Christian should pay. It is possible, in some situations, for it to be a serious reflection on a Christian if he is too popular.

There can be no doubt that popularity should not be the chief thing sought by a Christian. Too strong a desire for popularity frequently will lead to compromise. Those who have accomplished worthwhile things often have had to stand against the crowd; they have had to do some things that many others have not approved. Life's supreme search should not be for popularity but for the will of God.

What For?

The rightness or wrongness of popularity for the Christian depends, to a large degree, upon the purposes for which he desires it and will use it. The Christian should not seek popularity for its own sake. It is doubtful if he should seek it at all. Whatever popularity comes to him should come as a natural result of the kind of life he lives.

Certainly, he should not want to be popular merely to satisfy his ego. The only kind of popularity he can justifiably desire will be a popularity that will increase his opportunities for service for God and for his fellow man.

What a Christian does with whatever popularity he has will determine largely whether it will be a curse or a blessing to him and to others. A Christian should use whatever influence he has for Christian purposes. He should seek to carry the spirit of Christ into every group he touches.

A Christian student we know was a star football player. He found that his athletic success increased his influence on the campus. He was so uncompromisingly and wholesomely Christian on the athletic field, in the classroom, and on the campus in general, that the entire campus was lifted to higher levels of Christian living during his stay as a student. His influence lingered years after he had left the campus. He was a good steward of his influence, of the popularity he had.

Today or Tomorrow?

Popularity for anyone—Christian or non-Christian—may be very uncertain and passing. Any athlete can testify to the truthfulness of this statement. Even the popularity of Jesus rose and fell. Doubtless many of the same people who welcomed him into Jerusalem with cries of "Hosanna!" were in the crowd, a few days later, that cried "Crucify him!"

The standing of Jesus in the world did not depend upon the attitude of the people toward him during the triumphal entry or during his arrest, trial, and crucifixion. He has stood through the centuries as the central, dominant personality of all history. He has been hated by some, devotedly loved by others, and respected by all who have had even a passing acquaintance with him. His influence has been abiding. One reason for this fact is that he stood for things that abide. To him the Father's will was the most important thing in life. It was to be done regardless of what people might think or do.

Much of the constructive, creative work of the world has been done by men and women who dared to do what they considered to be right, even if opposed by others. Our main question should not be "Will this be the popular thing to do?" but "Is this the right thing to do?" If it is right, then we can be sure that time and the Lord are on our side.

Positive and Negative

Here are a few closing suggestions, some negative, others positive, about popularity:

From the negative viewpoint:

We should never compromise on basic moral principles.

We should not seek to win friends by being weak but by being strong.

We should learn, however, to stand for what is right in such a way as not to offend needlessly.

We shall tend to irritate and lose the friendship of others if we are too dogmatic or have a holier-than-thou attitude.

From the more positive viewpoint:

We should watch our personal appearance, being careful that we keep ourselves attractive and neat.

We should do our best to be genuine and sincere at all times and under all sorts of conditions.

We should cultivate an interest in others and in what they are doing.

We should be unselfish, devoted to the welfare of others.

We should remember that there is no substitute for a genuine love for people, for all kinds of people.

We should be cheerful and should develop and maintain healthy attitudes toward life.

We should talk about our religion more than we do, but if we want to have much influence with our associates, we must walk our religion more than we talk it. The walking will make the talking more effective.

The main question is not "Have I succeeded or failed to be popular?" but rather "Have I succeeded or failed to use what influence I have for Christ and for Christian ends?"

19. Religion: Positive and Negative

The problems and issues discussed in Part II represent, in the main, what some choose to call the "negatives" of the Christian life. This study of "right or wrong" would not be complete without some emphasis on the more positive expressions of the Christian religion along with some consideration of the relation of the negative and positive aspects of the Christian life.

The Good Christian

Before we consider specifically these matters, it may be wise to attempt to answer the question "What makes one a good Christian?"

Some say that the good Christian is one who is sound or orthodox in his beliefs. In contrast, there are other people who say, "It makes little difference what you believe; it is what you do that counts."

As is usually true, somewhere between these two extremes is the best or correct position. It does make considerable difference what one believes about God, Christ, the Bible, man, sin, salvation, and the church. There is enough wrapped up potentially in our beliefs concerning these and closely related subjects to determine what we become, what will be the motivating drives in our lives, and what will be our contribution to the world.

However, the ultimate goodness and worth of a Christian involves more than what he believes. It is possible for him to be orthodox, at least theoretically, in his beliefs, while at the same time he may be a very poor example of what a Christian should be.

A second answer frequently given to the question "What makes one a good Christian?" is faithfulness to the formal requirements of his religion. In other words, one who is faithful in his attendance at the services of his church and gives liberally of his time, talents, and money to support and to promote the program of his church and the cause of Christ is judged to be a good Christian.

Such a person will usually be a good Christian. However, this is not necessarily true. There is even a possibility that an attempt may be made to substitute faithfulness to those formal requirements for a consistent Christian life.

A third general answer that is given to the question "Who is the good Christian?" is that he is the one who is active in the work of the Lord. Certainly every Christian should be active in some phase of the work of the Lord in his church and community. It is possible, however, for one to be extremely active and yet not be a good Christian.

Still another answer to the question "What makes one a good Christian?" is that it is the kind or quality of life he lives. Most of us will agree that this is the best answer to whether or not one is a real Christian. Jesus himself said, "You will know them by the way they act" (Matt. 7:16), while James said, "Show me how you can have faith without actions; I will show you my faith by my actions" (Jas. 2:18).

We should remember, however, that the best Christian will be sound in the faith. He will conscientiously observe the formal requirements of his religion. He will be active in the work of the Lord. In addition to these, he will live a consistent life for Christ.

There are two emphases that properly may be made concerning consistent Christian living: the negative and the positive. Some people tend to judge the Christian's life largely in terms of what he does not do, while others give primary emphasis to what he does or to the positive quality of life revealed in his day-by-day contacts with others.

Some, who give the positive emphasis first place, judge a man's religion largely in terms of his relation to other individuals, while others emphasize primarily his attitude toward and his work on behalf of certain social and moral issues of the day. Will you not agree that both of these will characterize a good Christian? His Christian life will express itself positively in relation to other individuals. But positive Christian living also calls for an effort to correct the problems of our world, the conditions that dwarf and twist the lives of people. A Christian should not only forsake wrong and do right; he should also work to right wrong. Many contemporary young people are at work attempting to improve housing, race relations, pollution, traffic safety, and slums. They are helping the poor, the nonreader, the aged, the sick, the imprisoned, the lonely, and others.

The Place of the Negative

What place does and should the negative emphasis have in the Christian life? We know, of course, that the "thou shalt nots" are very prominent in the Old Testament. All but two of the Ten Commandments are stated negatively.

Some Christians argue that we are no longer under the law, that we are under grace. They suggest that the negative emphasis belonged to the childhood period of the race. This may be correct. At least one sign of maturity is the fact that one accentuates or emphasizes the positive phases of life more and the negative less. But who would dare say that he is so mature that he no longer needs some emphasis on the negatives of the Christian life?

We shall not be prepared, however, to proceed to the more positive, mature type of Christian life unless we have had a real victory in the area of the negatives. The victories in that area are essential to the maturing process. Furthermore, it is possible that a decision not to do a certain thing may be, at that particular time, our most important decision. It may set the direction of our lives. At least we must be willing to follow the Lord in regard to the negatives of life if we expect him to find full expression in us and through us in the positive phases of our lives.

The Place of the Positive

Paul instructed his converts to put off some things but also to put on some things (see Col. 3:1–14). The final test of how mature we are as Christians is how much the spirit of Christ lives in us and finds expression through us in our relations with others. Do we have the qualities Paul says should characterize the one who has been raised with Christ? They are: "compassion, kindness, humility, gentleness, and patience." He then concludes, "And to all these add love, which binds all things together in perfect unity" (Col. 3:12–14). How much do we manifest the fruit of the Spirit, which is "love, joy, peace, patience, kindness, goodness, faithfulness, humility, and self-control" (Gal. 5:22–23)?

Let us emphasize again that the positive is the supreme test of the mature Christian life, although it is never to be substituted for the negative aspects of that life. Most negatives, as we mature, will disturb and concern us less and less. This will be true primarily because we have settled these matters. Have you observed that the Christians in your church who count for most in the church and in the community are those who no longer have to debate with themselves as to whether or not it is right or wrong for them to do most of the things that have been discussed in Part II? They have made decisions that are final for them concerning those things.

The preceding correctly implies a possible relationship between the settling of the negatives and the development of stable, positive, Christian character. Every decision we make concerning any negative phase of the Christian life will contribute, in one way or another, to the positive side of our Christian lives. On the other hand, as we develop along positive lines, we have a broader and sounder basis for decisions concerning these negative matters.

There is at least one other thing that we should remember about the maturing process of the Christian life. One test of how mature we are is how much of the expression of the positive Christian life flows naturally and inevitably from the vitality of an inner relationship with the living Christ.

We have not arrived at spiritual maturity until the spirit of Christ so lives in us that it finds normal and natural expression through our lives. As we mature, we become increasingly unconscious that our lives are influencing others for Christ. The best Christians are largely unconscious that they are good. Christ so lives in them that others cannot help but see him incarnated in their lives. He has become a well of living water within them, flowing through them to bless all they touch.

The preceding does not mean that we should cease all striving after goodness. No, so long as we are immature—and none of us ever reaches full maturity—we should make a conscious effort to live the Christian life. This we can do without any apology or embarrassment, knowing that it is the common lot of all Christians. Even Paul said:

I do not claim that I have already succeeded in this, or have already become perfect. I keep going on to try to possess it, for Christ Jesus has already possessed me. Of course, brothers, I really do not think that I have already reached it; my single purpose in life, however, is to forget what is behind me and do my best to reach what is ahead. So I run straight toward the goal in order to win the prize, which is God's call through Christ Jesus to the life above.

All of us who are spiritually mature should have this same attitude. If, however, some of you have a different attitude, God will make this clear to you. However that may be, let us go forward according to the same rules we have followed until now. (Phil. 3:12–16)

Incidentally, this passage is full of athletic terminology, drawn from the Greek races.

What does all of this mean to us? It simply means that we shall continue unto the end of our earthly journey to be immature spiritually, in some way and to some degree. Full maturity would mean perfection.

This, in turn, means that we shall need to give some attention indefinitely to the "thou shalt nots" of the Christian life. We shall have to keep on making decisions concerning things we should or should not do. It also means that we shall need to continue to put forth conscious effort to be a good Christian, to give Christ a chance to express himself more fully through us.

It means, however, that we can measure our progress toward maturity by the direction in which our lives are moving. Are the negatives of decreasing and the positive phases of the Christian life of increasing significance and importance to us? Is less and less conscious effort required for us to live a decent Christian life?

20. Victory over Temptations

There was a tradition among certain Indians that the spirit of one who was scalped entered into the warrior who scalped him. This supposedly made the warrior stronger and more courageous. Each victory gave additional strength for the next battle.

There is a sense in which this is true in life. There is a stanza of an old song which expresses a comparable idea:

> Yield not to temptation
> For yielding is sin:
> Each victory will help you
> Some other to win.

Some of the things discussed in the chapters of Part II may represent real temptations to you. How can you have the victory over them and over temptations in general?

Recognize Their Sources

One step and possibly the first one in a conquest of temptation is to recognize the possible sources of temptations. There is a sense in which God tests Christians or permits them to be tested, but he never tempts anyone to do evil (Jas. 1:13). God's pull on man is toward the good rather than the evil.

There are three main sources of temptations, all interrelated in a sense. A knowledge of these will help us to strive more intelligently and successfully for victory when tempted.

The first of these sources is the devil. It was he who approached Eve in the form of the serpent. "The Spirit led

Jesus into the desert to be tempted by the Devil" (Matt. 4:1). Paul advised the Ephesians to put on the armor that God gave them that they might be able to "stand up against the Devil's evil tricks" (Eph. 6:11).

Most temptations have their immediate source in the spoken invitation, the attitude, or the example of some person. This is the second of the three main sources of temptations. There are some people who deliberately seek to entice others into sin. These enticers make the temptation and the sin it would lead to as attractive as possible. They appeal to the young to come and have a "good time" but hide from them the ultimate consequences of sin.

The third main source of temptations is our own evil desires and weaknesses. Have you ever done anything wrong and immediately said to yourself, "That was not I; it must have been someone else?" All of us, at times, have the feeling that we are a Dr. Jekyll and a Mr. Hyde. There is something within us that responds to the appeal of the good or right; there is likewise something within us that responds to the appeal of the evil or wrong.

When one becomes a Christian the balance in his life is shifted toward the right and good, yet there continues to be something within him which can be appealed to by the evil. James says: "A person is tempted when he is drawn away and trapped by his own evil desires" (Jas. 1:14).

We cannot shift the responsibility for our temptations and sins to others. Although the temptation may come from outside ourselves, there is something within us that responds to it. The ultimate responsibility for our sins rests squarely upon us. We make our own decisions. Our will is ours with which to say yes or no.

Understand Their Purposes

The fact that God does not directly send temptations does not mean that he does not use them for his purposes. An understanding of the purposes for which God may use temptations will aid us, to a degree, in our effort to overcome them.

They cannot serve God's purposes, however, unless we have the victory over them.

Temptations, if overcome, will develop character. The athlete develops his body by exercise and by overcoming physical resistance; the scholar sharpens his mind by tackling difficult intellectual problems and solving them; the Christian grows character by overcoming the temptations of life.

Christians should be the most courageous of people. The problems, the difficulties, and the temptations of life should not be permitted to defeat them. Their problems should be made stepping stones to higher levels of living. The conquest of temptations is a part of the maturing process.

Temptations serve as a means of testing us. A leading tire manufacturer has the slogan "Tested on the speedway for your safety on the highway." There are highly skilled pilots who thoroughly test planes before they are released for military or commercial service. In this way, imperfections and weaknesses may be revealed.

In much the same way, character is revealed by testing. There is no way of being sure of a life, whether it is ours or another's, until that life has been thoroughly tested. Just as a strong, sturdy oak cannot be grown in a hothouse, so strong Christian character cannot be developed in a spiritual vacuum. The Christian, if he is to grow, must meet squarely and have the victory over the tests and challenges of life.

Temptations to a Christian can and should serve another good purpose. They should make us conscious of our need of divine help. The experiences we have with temptations prove to us that we fail when we attempt to meet in our own strength the challenges of the devil and our own corrupt nature. The wonderful thing, however, is that when we turn to our Heavenly Father for the necessary assistance, we always find him adequate.

Conditions for Conquest

If we expect to have progressively the victory over temptations, we must meet certain conditions.

One thing we can and should do is to avoid temptations whenever we can wisely do so. There may arise occasions when it would be cowardly not to face some temptation squarely, but it is foolhardy to place ourselves needlessly in situations that tempt us to do wrong. That is one count against some of the problems discussed in Part II. We should remember that Jesus taught his disciples to pray, "Do not bring us to hard testing, but keep us safe from the Evil One" (Matt. 6:13).

Although we may seek, in every legitimate way, to avoid temptations, we shall still face plenty of them. If we are to win out over them, we must believe that victory is possible.

Victories on the athletic field, in military combat, or in life's battles are won by those who believe they can win. Most battles, before they are fought, are decided within the minds and hearts of the combatants. Christians can be and should be victorious over temptations. We are not supposed to live defeated lives.

Jesus, in his contest with the devil, came out victor over each temptation. Luke, in closing his account of the temptation of Jesus, said: "When the Devil finished tempting Jesus in every way, he left him for a while" (Luke 4:13). Jesus had many temptations which are not recorded. He "was tempted in every way that we are, but did not sin" (Heb. 4:15). The writer adds: "Let us be brave, then, and come forward to God's throne, where there is grace. There we will receive mercy and find grace to help us just when we need it" (v. 16). Tempted "in every way" is our assurance of a sympathetic Savior; "but did not sin" is our assurance of victory. We have the strength of the Master at our command.

Paul, writing to the Christians in one of the most wicked cities of that time, said: "Every temptation that has come your way is the kind that normally comes to people. For God keeps his promise, and he will not allow you to be tempted beyond your power to resist; but at the time you are tempted he will give you the strength to endure it, and so provide you with a way out" (1 Cor. 10:13).

Another thing that will help us to have the victory is to remember Dad and Mother, our pastor and teacher, and our friends who have confidence in us and are depending upon us.

> I would be true, for there are those who trust me;
> I would be pure, for there are those who care;
> I would be strong, for there is much to suffer;
> I would be brave, for there is much to dare.

In addition to our loved ones and friends we can be sure that Jesus is depending upon us. When we remember what he has done for us, how can we as Christians be untrue to such a friend as he?

> Jesus is all the world to me,
> And true to Him I'll be;
> Oh, how could I this Friend deny,
> When He's so true to me?

An additional condition for victory is for us to keep busy doing good. Minds and hearts, hands and feet that are kept busy thinking and doing good will not have time to do evil. This "good" should include both activity for the Lord and fellowship with him. If we are busy in the church and wholesome school and community activities, the occasions for serious temptations will be greatly reduced. This will be particularly true if we take some time each day for fellowship with our Heavenly Father through Bible study, prayer, and meditation.

Still another condition for victory, which has already been suggested, is that we must fight against temptations when they come. The Christian life is a hotly contested game, a constant warfare. Victory cannot be expected without a fight. The Christian is to "oppose the Devil" (Jas. 4:7); to "struggle [an athletic term] against sin" (Heb. 12:4).

Standards of right and wrong and ideals of personal conduct should be carefully and prayerfully determined. These standards and ideals should be defended at any cost. The fight may be hard, but the victory will be worth it. God's assurance of victory is given only to the courageous, fighting heart. We can be certain God will do his part; will we do ours? Are we going to be weaklings, drifting along with whatever crowd we happen to be in, or are we going to have the grit and the courage to buck the crowd when that crowd is wrong? Our answer to the preceding question is very important.

Let us remember that drifters are never lifters. They never start a current in the opposite direction. Drifters are lost in the current. Lifters stand out from the crowd and become the leaders of men for God and righteousness.

We may meet all of the preceding conditions for conquest over temptation and yet fail because we do not let the Lord fight with us. His power alone is stronger than sin. "Where sin increased, God's grace increased much more" (Rom. 5:20). Paul prayed to the Lord three times to remove his thorn in the flesh, which more than likely was some physical handicap but which may have been a special temptation or besetting sin. The Lord's reply was, "My grace is all you need; for my power is strongest when you are weak" (2 Cor. 12:9). Peter, often tempted and tried, spoke from experience when he said, "The Lord knows how to rescue godly men from their trials" (2 Peter 2:9).

Victory will come to us when we want it enough to bow before the Lord and ask his help and have enough faith to believe that he can and will help. It is then that we can say with Paul, "I can do all things in him who strengthens me" (Phil. 4:13, RSV).